Building UIs with Wijmo

Build user interfaces quickly using widgets

Yuguang Zhang

PUBLISHING

BIRMINGHAM - MUMBAI

Building UIs with Wijmo

First published: September 2013

Production Reference: 1120913

Published by Packt Publishing Ltd.
Livery Place
35 Livery Street
Birmingham B3 2PB, UK.

ISBN 978-1-84969-606-7

www.packtpub.com

Cover Image by Suresh Mogre (suresh.mogre.99@gmail.com)

Credits

Author
Yuguang Zhang

Reviewers
Stephen J. Naughton

Ryan Pinto

Michaël Vanderheeren

Acquisition Editor
Kartikey Pandey

Commissioning Editor
Subho Gupta

Technical Editor
Anita Nayak

Project Coordinator
Joel Goveya

Proofreader
Lauren Harkins

Indexer
Priya Subramani

Graphics
Abhinash Sahu

Production Coordinator
Manu Joseph

Cover Work
Manu Joseph

About the Author

Yuguang Zhang has worked as a web developer in a number of small companies. Notable companies where he has worked at include SociaLabra, a social media company, and SmartPager, a startup in mobile paging. He has expertise in developing interactive client-side applications with Knockout. As a personal project, he built the first IDE that runs Python in the browser using Knockout and jQuery UI, that is `pythonfiddle.com`. In addition, he designed and programmed `fiddlesalad.com`, a multi-language playground for rapid frontend development built with CoffeeScript and Django.

About the Reviewers

Stephen J. Naughton has been programming since the early days of the BBC Micro on which he authored the "Plotter ROM", allowing users to print screen to a plotter when Inkjet and other color printers were just appearing. He has worked in the industry as a systems engineer for about 20 years and as a full-time developer in 2003. He has now been a Microsoft MVP for five years in the area of ASP.Net and especially in Dynamic Data. Stephen is freelance web developer specializing in LOB ASP.Net Dynamic Data and LightSwitch application development.

Ryan Pinto is a technology entrepreneur who becomes familiar with emerging technologies in a heartbeat and has a passion for clear and accurate documentation.

He has an intuitive awareness and understanding of Information and System Architecture, being able to effortlessly identify and manipulate the data structure of a product and tailor frontend user experience to its stakeholders. He is ever ready to put in extra efforts and has a passion for getting the job done right, on schedule, and on budget.

A graduate from the University of Waterloo's School of Computer Science and Department of English Language, Ryan strongly believes in quality code with concise documentation. He has architected software solutions and written technical reports for large post-secondary institutions and telecommunication organizations. Projects range from artificially intelligent, OO PHP/SQL Bayesian web applications, to interactive Flash ActionScript market research tools.

Ryan is currently a co-founder and technical lead at SociaLabra Inc., a fast growing company that builds, manages, and integrates niche social networks (NSNs). He is active in both pre and post-sales roles, from client consultancy and business problem definition to solution implementation and support. Whether Java or JavaScript, Native Mobile or Responsive Design, he uses the latest in development ideology and technology to build a customizable platform powering varied NSNs for a number of education, hospitality, sports, and health organizations.

Ryan's knowledge with respect to development is diverse, and it's clear that his passion for the field extends beyond the workplace.

Michaël Vanderheeren is both a strategic and technical consultant to international industry leaders where he assists in new product development and defining growth strategies. He has over five years experience with usability and interface design and software development in general. He holds both a Masters degree in Computer Sciences and an MBA in General Management and keeps a keen eye on technological developments and their application in innovation projects. He previously was involved in the Absolution theme development for both jQuery and Wijmo and optimizing JavaScript for embedded devices in the healthcare industry.

I would like to thank my partner, friends, and family for supporting me in developing my career and giving me the opportunity to stretch the boundaries of both technology and innovation. A special thanks to my partner for the countless discussions and feedback moment on both success stories and difficult periods.

www.PacktPub.com

Support files, eBooks, discount offers and more

You might want to visit www.PacktPub.com for support files and downloads related to your book.

Did you know that Packt offers eBook versions of every book published, with PDF and ePub files available? You can upgrade to the eBook version at www.PacktPub.com and as a print book customer, you are entitled to a discount on the eBook copy. Get in touch with us at service@packtpub.com for more details.

At www.PacktPub.com, you can also read a collection of free technical articles, sign up for a range of free newsletters and receive exclusive discounts and offers on Packt books and eBooks.

http://PacktLib.PacktPub.com

Do you need instant solutions to your IT questions? PacktLib is Packt's online digital book library. Here, you can access, read and search across Packt's entire library of books.

Why Subscribe?

- Fully searchable across every book published by Packt
- Copy and paste, print and bookmark content
- On demand and accessible via web browser

Free Access for Packt account holders

If you have an account with Packt at www.PacktPub.com, you can use this to access PacktLib today and view nine entirely free books. Simply use your login credentials for immediate access.

Table of Contents

Preface	**1**
Chapter 1: Getting Started with Wijmo	**5**
Setting up Wijmo	**5**
Installing Wijmo the quick way via a CDN	6
Installing Wijmo for development	9
Customizing jQuery UI for download	9
Downloading Wijmo	10
Installing jQuery UI for development	11
Installing Wijmo for development	11
Adding Wijmo to an HTML document	12
Wijmo licensing	13
Required background	**14**
Summary	**14**
Chapter 2: The Dialog Widget	**15**
Wijmo additions to the dialog widget at a glance	**15**
Adding custom buttons	18
Configuring the dialog widget's appearance	21
Loading external content	23
Summary	**24**
Chapter 3: Form Components	**25**
Checkbox	**25**
Radio buttons	**26**
Dropdown	**28**
ComboBox	**30**
InputDate	**31**
InputMask	**34**
Summary	**37**

Chapter 4: Working with Images — 39
Using the carousel widget — 39
Creating the carousel widget — 39
Configuring the carousel widget — 41
Using the display options to show multiple images — 42
Specifying the navigation options — 44
Adding the timer and autoplay — 46
Using the gallery widget — 46
Creating the gallery widget — 47
Playing videos in the gallery widget — 49
Using the lightbox widget — 50
Creating the lightbox widget — 51
Changing the lightbox widget's appearance — 52
Summary — 53

Chapter 5: Advanced Widgets — 55
Using the tooltip widget — 55
Positioning the tooltip widget — 56
Loading AJAX content in the tooltip widget — 57
Styling the tooltip widget — 58
Using the upload widget with the ProgressBar element — 60
Applying Wijmo themes to HTML5 videos — 62
Using the editor widget — 63
Using the editor widget with BBCode for forums — 63
Summary — 64

Chapter 6: Dashboard with WijmoGrid — 65
Introduction to MVVM — 65
Introduction to Knockout — 67
Building a rating system with Knockout — 68
Building the dashboard — 70
Sending a message with Knockout and Socket.IO — 71
Displaying messages on the Dashboard — 75
Summary — 77

Chapter 7: Wijmo Mobile — 79
Getting started with Wijmo mobile — 79
Setting up Wijmo mobile — 79
Obtaining jQuery mobile — 79
Installing jQuery mobile — 80
Using a mobile browser emulator — 81
Creating an expander widget — 82
Passing options to the expander widget — 82

Creating a ListView widget	**83**
Creating an AppView widget	**84**
Adding the AppView pages	86
Reusing non-mobile pages	87
Summary	**90**
Chapter 8: Extending Wijmo	**91**
Extending Wijmo Open	**91**
Modifying the Dialog widget	91
Modifying a Wijmo theme with ThemeRoller	94
Summary	**95**
Index	**97**

Preface

Wijmo is a new JavaScript library focusing on user interface widgets. It builds on jQuery UI, enhancing existing widgets, and adding new ones. In this book we examine the Wijmo widgets essential for web development. The useful configuration options for 15 widgets are covered along with their usage scenarios. Most of the chapters take a code recipe approach for tasks that occur often in web development. Whenever you come across a widget or user interface component that you've implemented before, chances are that Wijmo widgets have you covered. The chapters in this book are designed to get you started using the widgets in no time. On the other hand, *Chapter 6, Dashboard with Wijmo Grid*, takes a different approach in building an application and explaining how it works.

There is no need for going in sequence of the chapters if you're familiar with Wijmo. However, if you're experiencing Wijmo for the first time, I would recommend going in the same order as the chapters.

What this book covers

Chapter 1, Getting Started with Wijmo, introduces Wijmo, the steps to install it, and licensing.

Chapter 2, The Dialog Widget, explains Wijmo's features that can be added to the jQuery UI dialog widget.

Chapter 3, Form Components, examines the Wijmo widgets for forms.

Chapter 4, Working with Images, shows the common uses of the gallery, lightbox, and carousel widgets.

Chapter 5, Advanced Widgets, covers the tooltip, upload, video, and editor widgets.

Chapter 6, Dashboard with Wijmo Grid, builds an interactive application combining Knockout and Wijmo.

Chapter 7, Wijmo Mobile, sets up the development environment for mobile and introduces mobile views.

Chapter 8, Extending Wijmo, explains how to modify widgets and change the themes.

What you need for this book

You will need a text editor with JavaScript, CSS, and HTML syntax highlighting. Notepad++ on Windows or Textmate on Mac is sufficient. Developing with Wijmo does not require fancy editor features, such as auto-complete or warnings for JavaScript. The widgets are simple and easy to use.

Besides a text editor, you also need a web browser. An Internet Explorer version higher than Version 5, Firefox, Safari, or Chrome are all supported by Wijmo. You probably already have one installed and prefer one over another.

Who this book is for

The primary audience for this book are the web developers working on projects that require the use of ready-made widgets. jQuery UI lacks necessary components or features, whereas Wijmo provides both free, open source widgets, as well as a licensed option for more complex widgets. Since this book covers both the areas, developers working on open source projects can also benefit.

Since Wijmo is easy to use, many of the simpler examples can be understood by a beginner with JavaScript. When the previous condition is met, this book is the first book that a JavaScript beginner should read after learning jQuery. Learning how to use Wijmo widgets will reduce the unnecessary work of writing custom JavaScript.

Conventions

In this book, you will find a number of styles of text that distinguish between different kinds of information. Here are some examples of these styles, and an explanation of their meaning.

Code words in text, database table names, folder names, filenames, file extensions, pathnames, dummy URLs, user input, and Twitter handles are shown as follows: "The `widget` method returns the dialog HTML element."

A block of code is set as follows:

```
$("#dialog").wijdialog({captionButtons: {
  pin: { visible: false },
  refresh: { visible: false },
  toggle: { visible: false },
  minimize: { visible: false },
  maximize: { visible: false }
  }
});
```

When we wish to draw your attention to a particular part of a code block, the relevant lines or items are set in bold:

```
maximize: {visible: true, click: function () {
  alert('To enlarge text, click the zoom icon.')
}, iconClassOn: 'ui-icon-lightbulb'},
close: {visible: true, click: self.close, iconClassOn:
  'ui-icon-close'}
```

New terms and **important words** are shown in bold. Words that you see on the screen, in menus or dialog boxes, for example, appear in the text like this: "clicking the **Next** button moves you to the next screen".

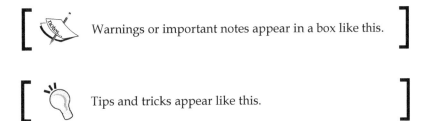

Warnings or important notes appear in a box like this.

Tips and tricks appear like this.

Reader feedback

Feedback from our readers is always welcome. Let us know what you think about this book—what you liked or may have disliked. Reader feedback is important for us to develop titles that you really get the most out of.

To send us general feedback, simply send an e-mail to feedback@packtpub.com, and mention the book title via the subject of your message.

If there is a topic that you have expertise in and you are interested in either writing or contributing to a book, see our author guide on www.packtpub.com/authors.

Customer support

Now that you are the proud owner of a Packt book, we have a number of things to help you to get the most from your purchase.

Downloading the example code

You can download the example code files for all Packt books you have purchased from your account at http://www.packtpub.com. If you purchased this book elsewhere, you can visit http://www.packtpub.com/support and register to have the files e-mailed directly to you.

Errata

Although we have taken every care to ensure the accuracy of our content, mistakes do happen. If you find a mistake in one of our books—maybe a mistake in the text or the code—we would be grateful if you would report this to us. By doing so, you can save other readers from frustration and help us improve subsequent versions of this book. If you find any errata, please report them by visiting http://www.packtpub. com/submit-errata, selecting your book, clicking on the **errata submission form** link, and entering the details of your errata. Once your errata are verified, your submission will be accepted and the errata will be uploaded on our website, or added to any list of existing errata, under the Errata section of that title. Any existing errata can be viewed by selecting your title from http://www.packtpub.com/support.

Piracy

Piracy of copyright material on the Internet is an ongoing problem across all media. At Packt, we take the protection of our copyright and licenses very seriously. If you come across any illegal copies of our works, in any form, on the Internet, please provide us with the location address or website name immediately so that we can pursue a remedy.

Please contact us at copyright@packtpub.com with a link to the suspected pirated material.

We appreciate your help in protecting our authors, and our ability to bring you valuable content.

Questions

You can contact us at questions@packtpub.com if you are having a problem with any aspect of the book, and we will do our best to address it.

1
Getting Started with Wijmo

Wijmo is composed of over 40 user interface widgets ranging from form components to enterprise charts. All of the widgets come with themes. The best features about Wijmo are:

- Wijmo is easy to use. It is a complete set of widgets with a wide array of configuration options. Chances are that Wijmo has a widget for every UI component you've used in your projects.

- It deals with implementation differences between browsers. All versions of IE since version 6 and other browsers are supported.

- It has Platinum support. Although the live phone support costs an annual fee, your team will never get stuck or experience downtime while working with Wijmo.

- It is open source and is hosted on a repository on GitHub with a GPL license for open source applications.

Not everything is perfect. Wijmo comes with its rough edges. In this book, I point out the pitfalls and guide you around them. The benefit of learning from this book is that you won't make the mistakes I've made. Learning Wijmo makes web development simpler, quicker, and more enjoyable.

Setting up Wijmo

Downloading and installing Wijmo only takes a few more steps compared to jQuery UI. It has files hosted on a content distribution network for a quick start. For this book, it is recommended that you download and set up the files for development. Since Wijmo is built on jQuery UI, I have included the details on obtaining and customizing jQuery UI. This chapter also covers how to install the minimized files for production environments.

Installing Wijmo the quick way via a CDN

Both jQuery and jQuery UI are hosted by Google and Microsoft on their **Content Distribution Networks (CDNs)**. The Microsoft service hosts standard jQuery UI themes as well as JavaScript. To use a CDN, you need to find the URLs of the files that you want first. Microsoft has a page listing their hosted libraries at `asp.net/ajaxlibrary/cdn.ashx`. If you click on the jQuery UI releases under the Table of Contents, several versions are listed. Clicking on a version will show you the URLs for the minified and regular versions. For example, jQuery UI 1.10.2 has the following URL:

`http://ajax.aspnetcdn.com/ajax/jquery.ui/1.10.2/jquery-ui.min.js`

The page also has a nice visual gallery of all the themes for the version, with the URL for the CSS theme below each theme. The URL for **Cupertino** is:

`http://ajax.aspnetcdn.com/ajax/jquery.ui/1.10.2/themes/cupertino/jquery-ui.css`

However, the reader is encouraged to select from one of the Wijmo themes, as they are more compatible with the library. Wijmo has a Theme Explorer (`http://wijmo.com/demo/themes/`) showcasing six themes (as of version 3.20131.1) as shown in the following screenshot:

The URL for the Rocket theme is:

`http://cdn.wijmo.com/themes/rocket/jquery-wijmo.css`

Wijmo provides a separate CSS for Widgets that change with each version. The URLs take the form: `http://cdn.wijmo.com/jquery.wijmo-pro.all.[version].min.css`. For the version at the time of writing this book, the form is: `http://cdn.wijmo.com/jquery.wijmo-pro.all.3.20131.1.min.css`.

The JavaScript files for Wijmo follow a similar format:

- `http://cdn.wijmo.com/jquery.wijmo-open.all.3.20131.1.min.js`
- `http://cdn.wijmo.com/jquery.wijmo-pro.all.3.20131.1.min.js`

To use Wijmo via a CDN, these URLs must be placed in script and link elements, as shown:

```
<!DOCTYPE HTML>
<html>
<head>
  <title>Example</title>
  <!--jQuery References-->
  <script src="http://code.jquery.com/jquery-1.9.1.min.js"
    type="text/javascript"></script>
  <script src="http://code.jquery.com/ui/1.10.1/jquery-ui.min.js"
    type="text/javascript"></script>
  <!--Wijmo Widgets JavaScript-->
  <script src=
    "http://cdn.wijmo.com/jquery.wijmo-open.all.3.20131.1.min.js"
      type="text/javascript"></script>
  <script src=
    "http://cdn.wijmo.com/jquery.wijmo-pro.all.3.20131.1.min.js"
      type="text/javascript"></script>
  <!--Theme-->
  <link href="http://cdn.wijmo.com/themes/aristo/jquery-wijmo.
css"rel="stylesheet" type="text/css" />
  <!--Wijmo Widgets CSS-->
  <link href="http://cdn.wijmo.com/jquery.wijmo-pro.all.3.20131.1.min.
css"rel="stylesheet" type="text/css" />
    <script id="scriptInit" type="text/javascript">
      $(document).ready(function () {
        $('#dialog').wijdialog({
          autoOpen: true,
          captionButtons: {
            refresh: { visible: false }
          }
```

```
        });
      });
    </script>
  </head>
  <body>
    <div id="dialog" title="Basic dialog">
      <p>Meet Wijmo.</p>
    </div>
  </body>
  </html>
```

If the Wijmo CDN files have been added properly, you should see a distinct "window" with the standard minimize, expand, and close buttons as shown in the following screenshot:

When browsers load JavaScript or CSS files, they check to see if the file is in the cache. If the user already has a cached version on his machine, then the browser loads from the cache instead of downloading the content. Serving jQuery over CDN will likely reduce the download size for the user. However, the Wijmo and jQuery UI libraries are less frequently used in web development so they are not likely to be cached. Instead of loading the full libraries from a CDN, creating a custom download with only the components used in your project, as covered in the next section, reduces the size. As a result, your web application will load faster.

Installing Wijmo for development

jQuery UI has five main areas of functionality. You can create a custom download that includes only the features necessary for your web application, resulting in a smaller library for browsers to download.

To avoid the pitfalls of using a jQuery UI theme, it is recommended to completely avoid the ThemeRoller on `http://jqueryui.com`. If Wijmo is configured with a jQuery UI theme such as Redmond, a few quirks will appear as show in the screenshot:

Customizing jQuery UI for download

The jQuery UI download page, `http://jqueryui.com/download/`, lets you select only the features required for your project to create a set of smaller files for the browser to download. This is usually a better idea than using a CDN, since jQuery UI has many releases each year and the chances of your project using the same version that the browser has already downloaded is low. For this book, download jQuery UI 1.10.2 with the default options. Later on, you will want to unselect the features that you don't use and see if your project still functions.

When customizing a jQuery UI library, the dependencies are sorted out for you. When a component is enabled, its dependencies are automatically selected. As you minimize your files for production, keep in mind that most of the effects along with some interactions and widgets may not be necessary. For example, only the **slide effect** is used in the accordion and dialog widgets. If your project only uses these widgets, then the other effects are not necessary.

Downloading Wijmo

To **start**, go to `http://wijmo.com/downloads/` and scroll down to the bottom. There is a navigation panel on the right-hand side with the **Downloads** link as shown in the following screenshot:

This loads the **Downloads** page, which consists of a list of ways to include Wijmo in your project along with an introductory video, **Get Started with Wijmo**, at the bottom. Click on the **Free Trial** button to download Wijmo Professional. The licensing options, along with a comparison chart of features, are at the end of this chapter. After clicking on the **Free Trial** button, you will need to register an account if you're a new user. Once you log in with your new account, you will see a link to download the library and you will be able to see a screen as shown in the following screenshot:

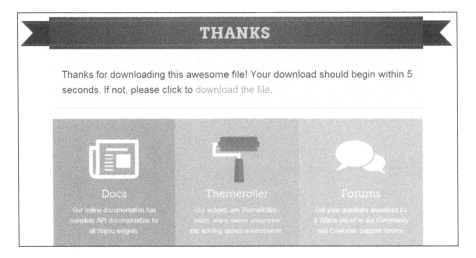

You will notice that there are JavaScript and CSS files for individual components and features in the `Wijmo` folder. They can be helpful when you want to reduce the size of the download for production. Since only the current version of Wijmo is downloadable from the website, you will want to keep a backup of your download.

Installing jQuery UI for development

Inside the jQuery UI download both the minified files for production and the uncompressed source code for development are present. Using the development versions makes it easy to debug, as you don't have to step through the minified code. To set up your development environment, copy the files `js\jquery-ui-1.10.2.custom.js` and `js\jquery-1.9.1.js` into a `lib` folder.

Installing Wijmo for development

Like the jQuery UI download, the Wijmo download contains all the files that you need for development and production. For this book, we will be using features in Wijmo Professional. Wijmo Professional depends on components in Wijmo Open. You need to copy the following files from the Wijmo download into the `lib` folder:

- `js\jquery.wijmo-open.3.20131.2.all.js`
- `js\jquery.wijmo-pro.all.3.20131.2.js`
- `css\jquery.open.css`
- `css\jquery.wijmo-pro.3.20131.2.css`
- `css\images`
- `Themes\rocket\jquery-wijmo.css`
- `Themes\rocket\images`

When copying the theme images, merge the folder contents. Note that the image paths are relative in the CSS and will work as long as you have the folder in the same directory as the CSS file. The Wijmo Professional files include the version number of the release that was downloaded. These change with each release, while the image and theme files are relatively static. The version, as of early 2013, is 3.20131.2. Simply replace it with your version number for the rest of the book or just use the version 3.20131.2.

Adding Wijmo to an HTML document

All that remains is to add Wijmo to your HTML document. You can do this by adding the script and link elements to the files in the lib folder as shown:

```html
<!DOCTYPE HTML>
<html>
<head>
  <title>Example</title>
  <!--jQuery References-->
  <script src="../lib/jquery-1.9.1.js"
    type="text/javascript"></script>
  <script src="../lib/jquery-ui.custom.js"
    type="text/javascript"></script>
  <!--Wijmo Widgets JavaScript-->
  <script src="../lib/jquery.wijmo-open.3.20131.2.all.js"
    type="text/javascript"></script>
  <script src="../lib/jquery.wijmo-pro.all.3.20131.2.js"
    type="text/javascript"></script>
  <!--Theme-->
  <link href="../lib/jquery-wijmo.css" rel="stylesheet"
    type="text/css" />
  <!--Wijmo Widgets CSS-->
  <link href="../lib/jquery.wijmo-open.3.20131.2.css"
    rel="stylesheet" type="text/css" />
  <link href="../lib/jquery.wijmo-pro.3.20131.2.css"
    rel="stylesheet" type="text/css" />
  <script id="scriptInit" type="text/javascript">
    $(document).ready(function () {
      $('#dialog').wijdialog({
        autoOpen: true,
        captionButtons: {
          refresh: { visible: false }
        }
      });
    });
  </script>
</head>
<body>
  <div id="dialog" title="Basic dialog">
    <p>Click OK to close this window.</p>
  </div>
</body>
</html>
```

Wijmo licensing

Wijmo Open is licensed under both MIT and GPL. The MIT license allows you to use the software in any way you want as long as the copyright attribution is kept. Wijmo Open is an expansion of jQuery UI with more widgets and options. A few of the widgets not included in jQuery UI that are in Wijmo Open are:

- Expander
- Radio Button
- TextBox
- DropDown
- CheckBox
- List
- Popup
- Splitter
- SuperPanel
- Video Player

Below the differences between jQuery UI and Wijmo are mentioned, showcasing which of the features are present in both or the other.

Wijmo Professional is intended for businesses developing closed-source projects. It includes everything from Wijmo Open, in addition to the following:

- Charts
- ComboBox
- Datasource
- Grid
- Input
    - Date
    - Mask
    - Number
- Media
    - Carousel
    - Gallery
    - Lightbox

- Pager
- Rating
- Tree
- Upload
- Wizard

The license cost is per developer at a rate of $495 (`https://wijmo.com/purchase/`). However, ComponentOne does offer a GPLv3 license for use in open source applications.

Required background

Before reading this book, you should be familiar with HTML, CSS, JavaScript, and jQuery. jQuery UI knowledge is not required, but would be a bonus since Wijmo is similar to jQuery UI in many ways. Only the last chapter of the book, which is based on extending Wijmo, requires advanced CSS and JavaScript knowledge. A basic working understanding of web development will get you through this book. If the examples in this chapter come naturally to you, then you're well on your way to learning Wijmo.

Summary

By this point, you should have the most recent version of Wijmo set up for development. If not, the source code for all the examples in this book are available at `https://github.com/yuguang/wijmo_essentials`. Download it to a permanent location on your computer and you will have all the code at your disposal. All of the examples are MIT licensed, so you may use it in any way you want.

Now that you have Wijmo set up on your computer for development, you are ready to start exploring Wijmo. In the next chapter, we dive into the dialog widget and look at several features which are not available in jQuery's version.

In addition to setting up Wijmo, we've also covered its licensing details. If you plan to use any of the complete Wijmo widgets in a proprietary application, make sure to get a license.

2
The Dialog Widget

The dialog widget is in the Wijmo Open set. It is an enhancement of the jQuery UI dialog with more features. Wijmo dialogs can be maximized, minimized, pinned to a location, and display external content from a URL in the dialog window. This chapter discusses the options, methods, and events that are added in Wijmo, and how to use them to change the appearance and behavior of the dialog.

Wijmo additions to the dialog widget at a glance

By default, the dialog window includes the pin, toggle, minimize, maximize, and close buttons. Pinning the dialog to a location on the screen disables the dragging feature on the title bar. The dialog can still be resized. Maximizing the dialog makes it take up the area inside the browser window. Toggling it expands or collapses it so that the dialog contents are shown or hidden with the title bar remaining visible. If these buttons cramp your style, they can be turned off with the captionButtons option. You can see how the dialog is presented in the browser from the following screenshot:

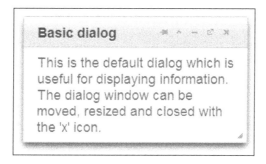

Wijmo features additional API compared to jQuery UI for changing the behavior of the dialog. The new API is mostly for the buttons in the title bar and managing window stacking. Window stacking determines which windows are drawn on top of other ones. Clicking on a dialog raises it above other dialogs and changes their window stacking settings. The following table shows the options added in Wijmo.

Options	Events	Methods
captionButtons	blur	disable
contentUrl	buttonCreating	enable
disabled	stateChanged	getState
expandingAnimation		maximize
stack		minimize
zIndex		pin
		refresh
		reset
		restore
		toggle
		widget

- The contentUrl option allows you to specify a URL to load within the window.
- The expandingAnimation option is applied when the dialog is toggled from a collapsed state to an expanded state.
- The stack and zIndex options determine whether the dialog sits on top of other dialogs.
- Similar to the blur event on input elements, the blur event for dialog is fired when the dialog loses focus.
- The buttonCreating method is called when buttons are created and can modify the buttons on the title bar.
- The disable method disables the event handlers for the dialog. It prevents the default button actions and disables dragging and resizing.
- The widget method returns the dialog HTML element.
- The methods maximize, minimize, pin, refresh, reset, restore, and toggle, are available as buttons on the title bar. The best way to see what they do is play around with them.

- In addition, the `getState` method is used to find the dialog state and returns either maximized, minimized, or normal.

- Similarly, the `stateChanged` event is fired when the state of the dialog changes.

The methods are called as a parameter to the `wijdialog` method. To disable button interactions, pass the string `disable`:

```
$("#dialog").wijdialog ("disable");
```

Many of the methods come as pairs, and `enable` and `disable` are one of them. Calling `enable` enables the buttons again. Another pair is `restore/minimize`. `minimize` hides the dialog in a tray on the left bottom of the screen. `restore` sets the dialog back to its normal size and displays it again.

The most important option for usability is the `captionButtons` option. Although users are likely familiar with the minimize, resize, and close buttons; the pin and toggle buttons are not featured in common desktop environments. Therefore, you will want to choose the buttons that are visible depending on your use of the dialog box in your project. To turn off a button on the title bar, set the `visible` option to `false`. A default jQuery UI dialog window with only the close button can be created with:

```
$("#dialog").wijdialog({captionButtons: {
  pin: { visible: false },
  refresh: { visible: false },
  toggle: { visible: false },
  minimize: { visible: false },
  maximize: { visible: false }
  }
});
```

The other options for each button are `click`, `iconClassOff`, and `iconClassOn`. The `click` option specifies an event handler for the button. Nevertheless, the buttons come with default actions and you will want to use different icons for custom actions. That's where `iconClass` comes in. `iconClassOn` defines the CSS class for the button when it is loaded. `iconClassOff` is the class for the button icon after clicking. For a list of available jQuery UI icons and their classes, see `http://jquery-ui.googlecode.com/svn/tags/1.6rc5/tests/static/icons.html`.

Our next example uses `ui-icon-zoomin`, `ui-icon-zoomout`, and `ui-icon-lightbulb`. They can be found by toggling the text for the icons on the web page as shown in the preceding screenshot.

Adding custom buttons

jQuery UI's dialog API lacks an option for configuring the buttons shown on the title bar. Wijmo not only comes with useful default buttons, but also lets you override them easily.

```
<!DOCTYPE HTML>
<html>
<head>
  ...
  <style>
    .plus {
      font-size: 150%;
    }
  </style>
  <script id="scriptInit" type="text/javascript">
    $(document).ready(function () {
      $('#dialog').wijdialog({
        autoOpen: true,
```

```
      captionButtons: {
      pin: { visible: false },
      refresh: { visible: false },
      toggle: {visible: true, click: function () {
        $('#dialog').toggleClass('plus')
      }, iconClassOn: 'ui-icon-zoomin', iconClassOff:
        'ui-icon-zoomout'},
      minimize: { visible: false },
      maximize: {visible: true, click: function () {
      alert('To enloarge text, click the zoom icon.')
      }, iconClassOn: 'ui-icon-lightbulb'},
      close: {visible: true, click: self.close, iconClassOn:
        'ui-icon-close'}
      }
    });
    });
  </script>
</head>
<body>
  <div id="dialog" title="Basic dialog">
    <p>Loremipsum dolor sitamet, consectetueradipiscingelit.
      Aeneancommodo ligula eget dolor.Aeneanmassa. Cum
      sociisnatoquepenatibusetmagnis dis parturient montes,
      nasceturridiculus mus. Donec quam felis, ultriciesnec,
      pellentesqueeu, pretiumquis, sem.
      Nullaconsequatmassaquisenim. Donecpedejusto, fringillavel,
      aliquetnec, vulputate</p>
  </div>
</body>
</html>
```

We create a dialog window passing in the `captionButtons` option. The pin, refresh, and minimize buttons have `visible` set to `false` so that the title bar is initialized without them. The final output looks as shown in the following screenshot:

In addition, the toggle and maximize buttons are modified and given custom behaviors. The toggle button toggles the font size of the text by applying or removing a CSS class. Its default icon, set with `iconClassOn`, indicates that clicking on it will zoom in on the text. Once clicked, the icon changes to a zoom out icon. Likewise, the behavior and appearance of the maximize button have been changed. In the position where the maximize icon was displayed in the title bar previously, there is now a lightbulb icon with a tip.

Although this method of adding new buttons to the title bar seems clumsy, it is the only option that Wijmo currently offers. Adding buttons in the content area is much simpler. The `buttons` option specifies the buttons to be displayed in the dialog window content area below the title bar. For example, to display a simple confirmation button:

```
$('#dialog').wijdialog({buttons: {ok: function () {
    $(this).wijdialog('close')
}}});
```

The text displayed on the button is `ok` and clicking on the button hides the dialog. Calling `$('#dialog').wijdialog('open')` will show the dialog again.

Configuring the dialog widget's appearance

Wijmo offers several options that change the dialog's appearance including title, height, width, and position. The title of the dialog can be changed either by setting the title attribute of the div element of the dialog, or by using the title option. To change the dialog's theme, you can use CSS styling on the wijmo-wijdialog and wijmo-wijdialog-captionbutton classes:

```
<!DOCTYPE HTML>
<html>
<head>
  ...
  <style>
    .wijmo-wijdialog {

      /*rounded corners*/
      -webkit-border-radius: 12px;
      border-radius: 12px;
      background-clip: padding-box;

      /*shadow behind dialog window*/
      -moz-box-shadow: 3px 3px 5px 6px #ccc;
      -webkit-box-shadow: 3px 3px 5px 6px #ccc;
      box-shadow: 3px 3px 5px 6px #ccc;

      /*fade contents from dark gray to gray*/
      background-image: -webkit-gradient(linear, left top, left
        bottom, from(#444444), to(#999999));
      background-image: -webkit-linear-gradient(top, #444444,
        #999999);
      background-image: -moz-linear-gradient(top, #444444,
        #999999);
      background-image: -o-linear-gradient(top, #444444, #999999);
      background-image: linear-gradient(to bottom, #444444,
        #999999);

      background-color: transparent;

      text-shadow: 1px 1px 3px #888;

    }
  </style>
  <script id="scriptInit" type="text/javascript">
```

```
    $(document).ready(function () {
      $('#dialog').wijdialog({width: 350});
    });
  </script>
</head>
<body>
  <div id="dialog" title="Subtle gradients">
    <p>Loremipsum dolor sitamet, consectetueradipiscingelit.
      Aeneancommodo ligula eget dolor.Aeneanmassa. Cum
      sociisnatoquepenatibusetmagnis dis parturient montes,
      nasceturridiculus mus. Donec quam felis, ultriciesnec,
      pellentesqueeu, pretiumquis, sem.
      Nullaconsequatmassaquisenim. Donecpedejusto, fringillavel,
      aliquetnec, vulputate
    </p>
  </div>
</body>
</html>
```

We now add rounded boxes, a box shadow, and a text shadow to the dialog box.
This is done with the `.wijmo-wijdialog` class. Since many of the CSS3 properties
have different names on different browsers, the browser specific properties are used.
For example, `-webkit-box-shadow` is necessary on Webkit-based browsers. The
dialog width is set to 350 px when initialized so that the title text and buttons all fit
on one line.

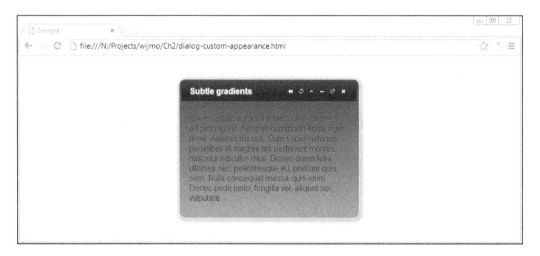

Loading external content

Wijmo makes it easy to load content in an iFrame. Simply pass a URL with the `contentUrl` option:

```
$(document).ready(function () {
  $("#dialog").wijdialog({captionButtons: {
    pin: { visible: false },
    refresh: { visible: true },
    toggle: { visible: false },
    minimize: { visible: false },
    maximize: { visible: true },
    close: { visible: false }
    },
  contentUrl: "http://wijmo.com/demo/themes/"
  });
});
```

This will load the Wijmo theme explorer in a dialog window with refresh and maximize/restore buttons. This output can be seen in the following screenshot:

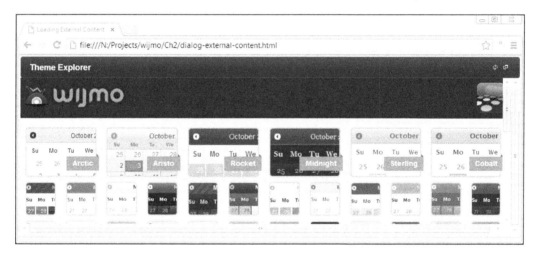

The refresh button reloads the content in the iFrame, which is useful for dynamic content. The maximize button resizes the dialog window.

Summary

The Wijmo dialog widget is an extension of the jQuery UI dialog. In this chapter, the features unique to Wijmo's dialog widget are explored and given emphasis. I showed you how to add custom buttons, how to change the dialog appearance, and how to load content from other URLs in the dialog.

3

Form Components

Wijmo form decorator widgets for radio button, checkbox, dropdown, and textbox elements give forms a consistent visual style across all platforms. There are separate libraries for decorating the dropdown and other form elements, but Wijmo gives them a consistent theme. jQuery UI lacks form decorators, leaving the styling of form components to the designer. Using Wijmo form components saves time during development and presents a consistent interface across all browsers. To use these form components with custom styles, see *Chapter 8, Extending Wijmo*.

Checkbox

The checkbox widget is an excellent example of the style enhancements that Wijmo provides over default form controls. The checkbox is used if multiple choices are allowed. The following screenshot shows the different checkbox states:

Wijmo adds rounded corners, gradients, and hover highlighting to the checkbox. Also, the increased size makes it more usable. Wijmo checkboxes can be initialized to be checked. The code for this purpose is as follows:

```
<!DOCTYPE HTML>
<html>
<head>
```

```
...
<script id="scriptInit" type="text/javascript">
  $(document).ready(function () {
    $("#checkbox3").wijcheckbox({checked: true});
    $(":input[type='checkbox']:not(:checked)").wijcheckbox();
  });
</script>
<style>
div {
  display: block; margin-top: 2em;
  }
</style>
</head>
<body>
  <div><input type='checkbox' id='checkbox1' /><label
    for='checkbox1'>Unchecked</label></div>
  <div><input type='checkbox' id='checkbox2' /><label
    for='checkbox2'>Hover</label></div>
  <div><input type='checkbox' id='checkbox3' /><label
    for='checkbox3'>Checked</label></div>
</body>
</html>.
```

In this instance, `checkbox3` is set to **Checked** as it is initialized.

 You will not get the same result if one of the checkboxes is initialized twice. Here, we avoid that by selecting the checkboxes that are not checked after `checkbox3` is set to be **Checked**.

Radio buttons

Radio buttons, in contrast with checkboxes, allow only one of the several options to be selected. In addition, they are customized through the HTML markup rather than a JavaScript API. To illustrate, the checked option is set by the `checked` attribute:

```
<input type="radio" checked />
```

jQuery UI offers a button widget for radio buttons, as shown in the following screenshot, which in my experience causes confusion as users think that they can select multiple options:

The Wijmo radio buttons are closer in appearance to regular radio buttons so that users would expect the same behavior, as shown in the following screenshot:

Wijmo radio buttons are initialized by calling the `wijradiomethod` method on radio button elements:

```
<!DOCTYPE html>
<html>
<head>
  ...
  <script id="scriptInit" type="text/javascript">
    $(document).ready(function () {
      $(":input[type='radio']").wijradio({
        changed: function (e, data) {
          if (data.checked) {
            alert($(this).attr('id') + ' is checked')
          }
        }
      });
    });
</script>
</head>
<body>
  <div id="radio">
  <input type="radio" id="radio1" name="radio"/><label
    for="radio1">Choice 1</label>
  <input type="radio" id="radio2" name="radio"
    checked="checked"/><label for="radio2">Choice 2</label>
  <input type="radio" id="radio3" name="radio"/><label
    for="radio3">Choice 3</label>
  </div>
</body>
</html>
```

In this example, the `changed` option, which is also available for checkboxes, is set to a handler. The handler is passed a `jQuery.Event` object as the first argument. It is just a JavaScript event object normalized for consistency across browsers. The second argument exposes the state of the widget. For both checkboxes and radio buttons, it is an object with only the `checked` property.

Dropdown

Styling a dropdown to be consistent across all browsers is notoriously difficult. Wijmo offers two options for styling the HTML `select` and `option` elements. When there are no option groups, the `ComboBox` is the better widget to use. This is covered in the next section. For a dropdown with nested options under option groups, only the `wijdropdown` widget will work. As an example, consider a country selector categorized by continent:

```
<!DOCTYPE HTML>
<html>
<head>
  ...
  <script id="scriptInit" type="text/javascript">
    $(document).ready(function () {
    $('select[name=country]').wijdropdown();
      $('#reset').button().click(function(){
        $('select[name=country]').wijdropdown('destroy')
        });
      $('#refresh').button().click(function(){
        $('select[name=country]').wijdropdown('refresh')
      })
    });
  </script>
</head>
<body>
  <button id="reset">
    Reset
  </button>
  <button id="refresh">
    Refresh
  </button>
  <select name="country" style="width:170px">
    <optgroup label="Africa">
    <option value="gam">Gambia</option>
    <option value="mad">Madagascar</option>
```

```
      <option value="nam">Namibia</option>
      </optgroup>
      <optgroup label="Europe">
      <option value="fra">France</option>
      <option value="rus">Russia</option>
      </optgroup>
      <optgroup label="North America">
      <option value="can">Canada</option>
      <option value="mex">Mexico</option>
      <option selected="selected" value="usa">United
        States</option>
      </optgroup>
   </select>
</body>
</html>
```

The select element's width is set to 170 pixels so that when the dropdown is initialized, both the dropdown menu and items have a width of 170 pixels. This allows the **North America** option category to be displayed on a single line, as shown in the following screenshot. Although the dropdown widget lacks a width option, it takes the select element's width when it is initialized. To initialize the dropdown, call the wijdropdown method on the select element:

```
$('select[name=country]').wijdropdown();
```

The dropdown element uses the blind animation to show the items when the menu is toggled.

Also, it applies the same click animation as on buttons to the slider and menu:

To reset the dropdown to a select box, I've added a reset button that calls the `destroy` method. If you have JavaScript code that dynamically changes the styling of the dropdown, the `refresh` method applies the Wijmo styles again.

ComboBox

The Wijmo ComboBox works on the `select` and `option` elements. The options can either be loaded through HTML markup or JavaScript Object Notation (JSON). For our example, we load the menu items by using markup:

```
<!DOCTYPE HTML>
<html>
<head>
  ...

  <script id="scriptInit" type="text/javascript">
    $(document).ready(function () {
      $("#states").wijcombobox({
        dropdownHeight: 150,
        dropdownWidth: 200,
        showingAnimation: { effect: "clip" },
        hidingAnimation: { effect: "fade" }
      });
      $("#states").bind("wijcomboboxselectedindexchanged",
        function(e, data) {
      $('#message').text('You moved from ' + data.oldItem.label +
        ' to ' + data.selectedItem.label + '.');
      } )
    });
  </script>
</head>
<body>
  <p><label id="output">Where do you live? (type to
    autocomplete)</label></p>
  <div>
```

```
      <select id="states">
      <option value="AL">Alabama</option>
         ...
      <option value="WY">Wyoming</option>
      </select>
   </div>
   <p id="message"></p>
</body>
</html>
```

The `showingAnimation` method specifies the animation to use when the options become visible. All of the jQuery UI effects can be used, and you can try them on the jQuery UI effects demo page: `http://jqueryui.com/effect/`. For the `hidingAnimation` method, I use the fade effect, which gradually decreases the opacity to 0. We bind to the event type `wijcomboboxselectedindexchanged` that is triggered when the selected index of the ComboBox is changed to display a message involving the old item and the new item.

InputDate

The InputDate widget provides a convenient visual mechanism for helping users to select dates. This widget supports a wide range of date formats, making it easier for the user to select a date and provide the information to you in a consistent way. The InputDate widget only works on an `input` element. To display a calendar without the `input` element, use the calendar widget, which looks as shown in the following screenshot:

To display an InputDate widget with a button to trigger the calendar, wrap the `input` element in a fixed width block, initialize the widget with the `showTrigger` option, and remove the `wijmo-wijinput-trigger` class:

```
<!DOCTYPE HTML>
<html>
<head>
  <title>InputDate Example</title>
  ...
$(document).ready(function () {
  $("#calendarInput").wijinputdate({showTrigger: true});

});
</script>
  <style>
    .date {
      width: 200px;
    }
</style>
</head>
<body>
  <div class="date"><input type="text" id="calendarInput" /></div>
</body>
</html>.
```

Similarly, showing an InputDate with a spinner for incrementing or decrementing the day, month, and year fields needs extra configuration. While the `input` field still accepts keystrokes that are valid within the date format, the spinner gives another option. Clicking once on the spinner changes the value of the selected date segment by one. Holding the click gradually accelerates the rate at which the date segment changes. Try it for yourself to get a feel of the visual effect:

```
<!DOCTYPE HTML>
<html>
<head>
  ...
  <script id="scriptInit" type="text/javascript">
    $(document).ready(function () {
      $spinnerInput = $("#spinnerInput");
```

```
    $spinnerInput.wijinputdate({showSpinner: true, dateFormat:
      'g', activeField: 3});
  });
</script>
</head>
<body>
  <div class="date"><input type="text" id="spinnerInput" /></div>
</body>
</html>
```

When working with a date input field, the most important part is sending the date to the server. Wijmo offers a variety of dateFormat options depending on your server setup and the date format that it accepts. In particular, if your server accepts the short date (mm/dd/yyyy) and short time (hh:mmtt) formats, then the general date format g will work for you. Simply initialize the InputDate widget with the dateFormat option set to g. With the previous example, it would be:

```
$spinnerInput.wijinputdate({showSpinner: true, dateFormat: 'g'});
```

 To get the date from the input, call the getText method:
$spinnerInput.wijinputdate("getText")
which returns the text displayed in the input box.

The wijinput format string follows the same convention as Java's SimpleDateFormat class, except for the AM/PM designator. The following table summarizes the formatting options:

Letter	Date or Time Component	Example	Output
y	Year	yyyy; yy	1996; 96
M	Month in year	MMMM;MMM;MM	July;Jul;07
d	Day in month	dd	10
H	Hour in day (0-23)	H	0
h	Hour in am/pm (1-12)	hh	12
m	Minute in hour	mm	30
s	Second in minute	ss	55
t	AM/PM	tt	AM

To illustrate, if the dateFormat is set as MMM-dd-yyyy, you can expect to see a date of the form Jul-14-2013 in the field.

InputMask

The InputMask widget shows the user the correct format for an input box. In addition, it prevents invalid input and gives visual cues about the data required. An example is shown as follows:

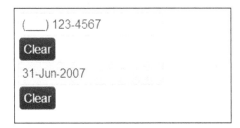

The input format is specified by a mask. A list of options are available on `http://wijmo.com/wiki/index.php/InputMask`. For our example, we make an input mask for U.S. phone numbers where the area codes are optional. These optional characters can be left blank:

```
<!DOCTYPE HTML>
<html>
<head>
  ...
  <script id="scriptInit" type="text/javascript">
    $(document).ready(function () {
      $("#textbox1").wijinputmask({
        mask: '(999) 000 - 0000'
      });
    });
  </script>
</head>
<body>
  <input type="text" id="textbox1" />
</body>
</html>
```

The masking element 9 indicates an optional digit, while 0 indicates a required digit. Literals such as the dash and parenthesis are displayed as they appear in the mask. By default, invalid inputs do not show up in the input element. To give the user feedback when the input is invalid, we add an error CSS class that is triggered on such inputs:

```
<!DOCTYPE HTML>
<html>
```

```
<head>
  ...
  <script id="scriptInit" type="text/javascript">
    $(document).ready(function () {
      $("#phoneNumber").wijinputmask({
        mask: '(999) 000-0000',
        resetOnSpace: true,
        invalidInput: function () {
          $("#phoneNumber").addClass('error')
        },
        textChanged: function () {
          $("#phoneNumber").removeClass('error')
        }
      });
    });
  </script>
<style>
  .error {
    border:1px solid red;
  }
  .mask {
  width: 130px;
  }
</style>
</head>
<body>
  <div class="mask"><input type="text" id="phoneNumber" /> </div>
</body>
</html>
```

When the text changes, we remove the error class. On invalid input, we add the class again. Another useful input mask is the day, month abbreviation, and year format as shown in the following screenshot:

This can be done with the input mask `00->L<LL-0000` where `>L` indicates an uppercase character from A to Z and `<LL` indicates two lowercase characters from a to z. To add a `clear` button for each of the fields, call the jQuery UI button function and register the click event on it. Since the clear button is placed next to the input, we call the `setText` method on its sibling input element.

```
<!DOCTYPE HTML>
<html>
<head>
  ...
  <script id="scriptInit" type="text/javascript">
    $(document).ready(function () {
      $("#phoneNumber").wijinputmask({
        mask: '(999) 000-0000',
        resetOnSpace: true,
        invalidInput: function () {
          $("#phoneNumber").addClass('error')
        },
        textChanged: function () {
          $("#phoneNumber").removeClass('error')
        }
      });
        $("#date").wijinputmask({
          mask: '00->L<LL-0000',
          resetOnSpace: true
        });
        $("button").button().click(function () {
          $(this).siblings().find("input").wijinputmask("setText",
            "");
        })
      });
  </script>
<style>
  .error {
    border:1px solid red;
  }
  .mask {
      width: 130px;
  }
  .ui-button-text-only .ui-button-text {
    padding: 3px 5px;
  }
</style>
```

```
</head>
<body>
  <div class="mask"><input type="text" id="phoneNumber" /><button
    class="reset">Clear</button></div>
  <div class="mask"><input type="text" id="date" /><button
    class="reset">Clear</button></div>
</body>
</html>
```

Note that we also override the CSS for the button padding so that the buttons are the same size as the inputs. With the `reset` button beside each field, the user would not need to fill out the form again if they make a mistake on one of the fields.

Summary

In this chapter we learned about Wijmo's form components. A checkbox is used when multiple items can be selected. Wijmo's checkbox widget has style enhancements over the default checkboxes. Radio buttons are used when only one item is to be selected. While jQuery UI only supports button sets on radio buttons, Wijmo's radio buttons are much more intuitive. Wijmo's dropdown widget should only be used when there are nested or categorized `<select>` options. The ComboBox comes with more features when the structure of the options is flat. InputDate is used to display a date selector calendar widget, while the InputMask is meant to give users a hint of what the correct input format is.

Now that you have learned the form components in Wijmo, try building a form on your own before moving onto the next chapter. Try making a nested form where selecting a choice in a radio group shows or hides fields.

4
Working with Images

This chapter introduces the widgets for working with images: the **carousel**, **gallery**, and **lightbox**. The carousel is a simpler form of the gallery widget, without thumbnails by default. Both of them are used to display a list of images on the page. The carousel is intended to show multiple images at once. The lightbox works differently in that it shows a selected image in full size and opens in a dialog on top of the page contents.

Using the carousel widget

The carousel widget displays a list of images. The images by default are aligned horizontally with previous and next buttons to scroll through them. Captions can be displayed at the bottom of each of the images. In the sections that follow, I'll show you how to create, configure, and use the carousel widget.

Creating the carousel widget

To set up the carousel widget, the width and height of the container element needs to be the same as the image sizes. For instance, if your images are 300 x 200, then the width and height needs to be set in the CSS as follows:

```
<!DOCTYPE HTML>
<html>
<head>
  ...
  <script id="scriptInit" type="text/javascript">
    $(document).ready(function () {
```

```
      $("#wijcarousel").wijcarousel({
        orientation: "horizontal",
        display: 1
      });
    });
  </script>
  <style type="text/css">
    #wijcarousel
    {
      width: 300px;
      height: 200px;
    }
  </style>
</head>
<body>
  <div id="wijcarousel">
    <ul>
      <li>
        <img alt="1" src="http://lorempixum.com/300/200/nature/1"
          title="Word1"/><span>Word Caption 1</span></li>
      <li>
        <img alt="2" src="http://lorempixum.com/300/200/nature/2"
          title="Word2" /><span>Word Caption 2</span></li>
      <li>
        <img alt="3" src="http://lorempixum.com/300/200/nature/3"
          title="Word3"/><span>Word Caption 3</span></li>
      <li>
        <img alt="4" src="http://lorempixum.com/300/200/nature/4"
          title="Word4"/><span>Word Caption 4</span></li>
      <li>
        <img alt="5" src="http://lorempixum.com/300/200/nature/5"
          title="Word5"/><span>Word Caption 5</span></li>
      <li>
        <img alt="6" src="http://lorempixum.com/300/200/nature/6"
          title="Word6" /><span>Word Caption 6</span></li>
    </ul>
  </div>
</body>
</html>
```

With these settings, one image is displayed at a time with next and previous buttons on the sides of the image, as shown in the following screenshot:

All of the images used in the example are the same size. This allows us to set the container dimensions without cropping or resizing the images.

Configuring the carousel widget

The carousel widget supports a number of settings that let you control the features available in the user interface as well as its display. The most useful ones are shown as follows:

Setting	Description
display	This setting specifies the number of images shown
step	This setting specifies the number of images scrolled by a transition
orientation	This setting specifies whether to scroll the images horizontally or vertically
showTimer	This setting allows the images in carousel to be played with a timer displaying the progress and a play/pause button
loop	This setting allows cycling to continue through the images so that the last image returns to the first one

The following diagram shows the different parts of the carousel widget:

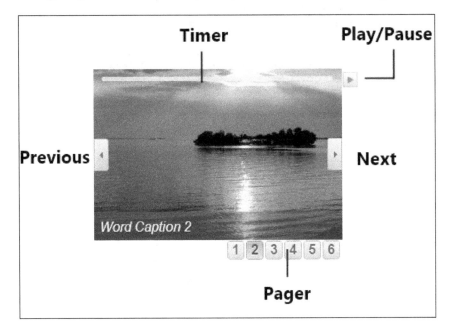

Using the display options to show multiple images

To show multiple images with the carousel widget, we increase the width of the `wijcarousel` element proportional to the number of images to show. Since each image is 300 pixels wide, to show two images at a time, we would set the display option to 2 and the width of the element to 600 pixels. As another example, to show three images at a time, we set the display options and CSS as shown in the code listing:

```
<!DOCTYPE HTML>
<html>
<head>
  ...
  <script id="scriptInit" type="text/javascript">
    $(document).ready(function () {
      $("#wijcarousel").wijcarousel({
        orientation: "horizontal",
        display: 3,
```

```
        step: 2
      });
    });
  </script>
<style type="text/css">
  #wijcarousel
  {
    width: 900px;
    height: 200px;
  }
</style>
</head>
<body>
  <div id="wijcarousel">
  <ul>
    <li>
      <img alt="1" src="http://lorempixum.com/300/200/nature/1"
        title="Word1" /><span>Word Caption 1</span></li>
      <li>
      <img alt="2" src="http://lorempixum.com/300/200/nature/2"
        title="Word2" /><span>Word Caption 2</span></li>
    <li>
      <img alt="3" src="http://lorempixum.com/300/200/nature/3"
        title="Word3" /><span>Word Caption 3</span></li>
    <li>
      <img alt="4" src="http://lorempixum.com/300/200/nature/4"
        title="Word4" /><span>Word Caption 4</span></li>
    <li>
      <img alt="5" src="http://lorempixum.com/300/200/nature/5"
        title="Word5" /><span>Word Caption 5</span></li>
    <li>
      <img alt="6" src="http://lorempixum.com/300/200/nature/6"
        title="Word6" /><span>Word Caption 6</span></li>
    </ul>
  </div>
</body>
</html>
```

As you can see in the following screenshot, setting the width to 900 pixels allows enough room for the next and previous buttons so that they do not overlap with the images.

We also set the `step` property in the options to `2` so that hitting the next button slides the current images to the left so that two of them disappear. Wijmo plays a nice animation while sliding the third image into the position of the first image. To try out various animation and options, head to `http://wijmo.com/demo/explore/?widget=Carousel&sample=Animation`.

Specifying the navigation options

In addition to the next and previous buttons, a pager can be added to navigate to a specific image. The pager comes in many forms, specified by the `pagerType` option. The available options are numbers, dots, thumbnails, and a slider. If you want to use thumbnails, I recommend switching to the gallery widget as it comes with thumbnails by default. The gallery widget is covered in the next section. The position settings for a pager, as well as other elements, have fields that position elements relative to each other.

For a visual display of the position options, refer to the section *Positioning the Tooltip* in the next chapter. In this example, we place the pager's center top at the bottom of the carousel with the `my` option and move it left by 10 pixels with the offset:

```
pagerPosition: {
  my: "center top",
  at: "center bottom",
  offset: "-10 0"
}
```

Another handy option to make the carousel look cleaner is to display buttons on the outside instead of overlapping them with the image.

Putting it all together, we initialize the carousel widget with the pager as follows:

```
$("#wijcarousel").wijcarousel({
  orientation: "horizontal",
  display: 1,
  showPager: true,
  pagerPosition: {
    my: "center top",
    at: "center bottom",
    offset: "-10 0"
  },
  pagerType: "dots",
  buttonPosition: "outside"
});
```

To center align the carousel, a common pattern is to set the width and let the margins be automatically adjusted:

```
#wijcarousel
{
  display: block;
  margin: 0 auto;
  width: 304px;
  height: 200px;
}
```

The end result is a user friendly, clean interface as shown in the following screenshot:

Adding the timer and autoplay

To let the images play like a slideshow, we only need to set the `auto` option to `true`. Along with the `loop` option, the images can play continuously. If you have many images to show, you will want to reduce the interval or duration when each is shown. Furthermore, the `timer` option allows the user to pause the slideshow. The timer in progress looks like the one shown in the following screenshot:

An example setting to play each image for three seconds before moving onto the next one is listed as follows:

```
$("#wijcarousel").wijcarousel({
  orientation: "vertical",
  interval: 3000,
  loop: true,
  auto: true,
  showTimer: true,
  display: 1
});
```

Using the gallery widget

As mentioned in the section on the carousel widget, the gallery widget displays navigable thumbnails by default. Selecting a thumbnail shows a larger version of the image above it.

Creating the gallery widget

As you might expect by now, the Wijmo gallery widget is created with the `wijgallery` method:

```
$("#wijgallery").wijgallery({
  thumbsDisplay: 3
});
```

This gallery is created with as much reuse of the carousel example as possible. For the gallery, we only limit the width on the container as it needs space to display the thumbnails:

```
#wijgallery {
  width: 300px;
}
```

We set the number of thumbnails to 3 due to the horizontal area below our images. Wijmo automatically crops the images for the thumbnails. Our gallery widget now looks like the one shown in the following screenshot:

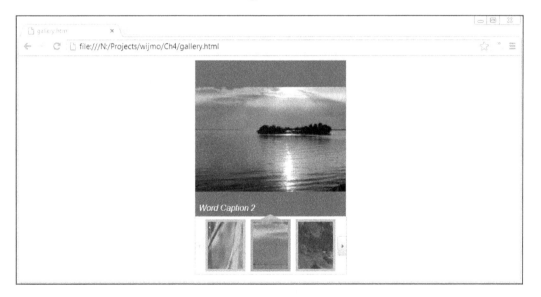

In the example, we used the same HTML list format as for the carousel. Nevertheless, the Wijmo documentation recommends another format:

```
<div id="wijgallery">
  <ul>
    <li><a href="http://lorempixum.com/300/200/nature/1">
    <img alt="1" src="http://lorempixum.com/100/100/nature/1"
      title="Word Caption 1"/>
    </a></li>
    <li><a href="http://lorempixum.com/300/200/nature/2">
    <img alt="2" src="http://lorempixum.com/100/100/nature/2"
      title="Word Caption 2"/>
    </a></li>
    <li><a href="http://lorempixum.com/300/200/nature/3">
    <img alt="3" src="http://lorempixum.com/100/100/nature/3"
      title="Word Caption 3"/>
    </a></li>
    <li><a href="http://lorempixum.com/300/200/nature/4">
    <img alt="4" src="http://lorempixum.com/100/100/nature/4"
    title="Word Caption 4"/>
    </a></li>
    <li><a href="http://lorempixum.com/300/200/nature/5">
    <img alt="5" src="http://lorempixum.com/100/100/nature/5"
      title="Word Caption 5"/>
    </a></li>
    <li><a href="http://lorempixum.com/300/200/nature/6">
    <img alt="6" src="http://lorempixum.com/100/100/nature/6"
      title="Word Caption 6"/>
    </a></li>
  </ul>
</div>
```

Although more verbose, this format allows us to specify the thumbnail images. Now each 300 x 200 image is accompanied by a 100 x 100 thumbnail. The gallery widget automatically resizes images to fit the display area. If you want to resize the images in your gallery widget without changing the aspect ratio, refer to a blog post by one of the developers at `http://wijmo.com/maintaining-aspect-ratio-in-wijgallery/`.

Playing videos in the gallery widget

To play videos within the gallery widget, you just need to specify a thumbnail of the video and a link to it. An example markup with three videos is:

```
<div id="wijgallery">
  <ul>
    <li><a
      href="http://www.youtube.com/v/0ZNSVMaPIUQ?version=3&amp;hl=en_US">
      <img width="120" height="90"
        src="http://i.ytimg.com/vi/0ZNSVMaPIUQ/0.jpg"></a>
    </li>
    <li><a
      href="http://www.youtube.com/v/4B22QGJoxZQ?version=3&amp;hl=en_US">
        <img width="120" height="90"
          src="http://i.ytimg.com/vi/4B22QGJoxZQ/0.jpg"></a>
    </li>
    <li><a
      href="http://www.youtube.com/v/bpPMAyAxO4Q?version=3&amp;hl=en_US">
        <img width="120" height="90"
          src="http://i.ytimg.com/vi/bpPMAyAxO4Q/0.jpg"></a>
    </li>
  </ul>
</div>
```

The thumbnails will display at the bottom of the gallery. To prevent Wijmo from cropping the thumbnails, we can set the `thumbsLength` option to the width of the image. Moreover, the `thumbsDisplay` option, which determines the number of thumbnails shown, needs to be adjusted. The mode can be set to `swf` for flash or `iframe` for other video types. Since we did not specify a caption for the video, we set the `showCaption` option to `false`:

```
$("#wijgallery").wijgallery({
  thumbsDisplay: 4,
  thumbsLength: 100,
  mode: "swf",
  showCaption: false
});
```

In this example, the thumbnails are assumed to be 100 pixels wide. An additional library is required to play flash videos. The `swfobject.js` library must be loaded before the `wijgallery` method is called. A Wijmo gallery configured to play YouTube videos is shown as follows:

Using the lightbox widget

The lightbox widget is a tool to give focus to images. It displays the current image on top of other page contents in a modal dialog. The Wijmo lightbox widget shares many common features with the carousel and gallery widgets, including the navigation buttons, timer, and caption area. The lightbox comes with default settings that show the control buttons on hover along with an image count. In addition, it also adds a close button to the top right corner.

Creating the lightbox widget

Unlike the gallery and carousel widgets, the lightbox requires options to be specified in the `rel` attribute of the `anchor` element. The following example shows the required elements and a script that creates the lightbox:

```
<!DOCTYPE HTML>
<html>
<head>
...
  <script id="scriptInit" type="text/javascript">
    $(document).ready(function () {
      $("#lightbox").wijlightbox();
    });
  </script>
  <style type="text/css">
    #lightbox {
      width: 600;
    }
  </style>
</head>
<body>
  <div id="lightbox" class="">
  <a href="http://lorempixum.com/600/400/nature/1"
    rel="wijlightbox[stock];player=img">
  <imgsrc="http://lorempixum.com/150/125/nature/1" title="nature
    1"/></a>
  <a href="http://lorempixum.com/600/400/nature/2"
    rel="wijlightbox[stock];player=img">
  <imgsrc="http://lorempixum.com/150/125/nature/2" title="nature
    2"/></a>
  <a href="http://lorempixum.com/600/400/nature/3"
    rel="wijlightbox[stock];player=img">
  <imgsrc="http://lorempixum.com/150/125/nature/3" title="nature
    3"/></a>
  </div>
</body>
</html>
```

The lightbox widget requires an `img` element inside an anchor element. Also, the `img` element needs to have a title, which is displayed as a caption. As you're familiar now, we set the `width` attribute of the lightbox to be the width of the image. When you call the `wijlightbox` method with no settings and click on one of the images, you get an image frame on top of the page contents as shown in the following screenshot:

Changing the lightbox widget's appearance

The lightbox by default shows navigation and close buttons when hovering over it; and play/pause buttons for slideshows are also available. To show these buttons, use the `ctrlButtons` option. You may also want to display the lightbox with a `modal` view by setting the `modal` option to `true`. To avoid having the navigation controls overlap with the images, set the `controlsPosition` property to `outside`:

```
$("#lightbox").wijlightbox({
  modal: true,
  controlsPosition: 'outside',
  ctrlButtons: 'play|stop'
});
```

The result is shown as follows:

Summary

In this chapter, we learned about the carousel widget, which is used for displaying multiple images, and how to configure it with display and navigation options. This chapter also introduced the animation and timer options available for the carousel. Next, we learned about the gallery widget and using it to play videos. Finally, this chapter concluded with a section on the lightbox widget.

5
Advanced Widgets

Wijmo includes many advanced widgets commonly used in web development. These components of applications are often implemented with libraries or plugins. In this chapter, we cover the tooltip, upload, video, and editor widgets. The main advantage of using these Wijmo widgets over other libraries for the developer is its consistent API. For the user, the interface components look more consistent.

Using the tooltip widget

Browsers, by default, display a textbox or balloon when hovering over image elements that have title attributes. To make these text balloons user friendly, Wijmo's tooltip widget uses JavaScript and CSS to enhance them. By default, Wijmo shows the text in the `title` attribute of the tooltip elements. Consider a simple example with an input element:

```
<input title="Instructions for the form go here" type="text" />
```

Calling `$("input[title]").wijtooltip()` generates a tooltip that shows when hovering over the element. In addition, the jQuery selector only applies the tooltip on those input elements that have titles. In this section, we explore how to position the tooltip, load AJAX content within it, and change its style.

Positioning the tooltip widget

Wijmo uses jQuery UI's position method which takes four main parameters:

Field	Values	Description
my	left/right/center/top/ bottom/center	The position on the element being moved
at	left/right/center/top/ bottom/center	The position on the target element to be aligned against
of	selector	The target element to be positioned against
offset	Integer	The x y offset that specifies how much to move horizontally and vertically

The syntax reads almost like a sentence. Suppose we wanted to position a box with ID move-it so that its top left is at the right bottom of the target; then we could use the position method in the following way:

```
$("#move-it").position({
    "my": "left top",
    "at": "right bottom",
    "of": $("#target")
});
```

The following screenshot depicts the elements in the preceding example as boxes:

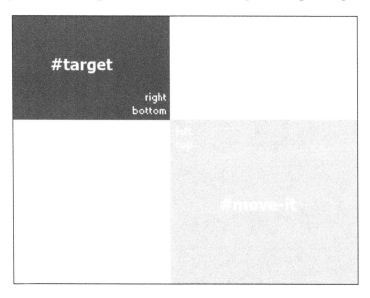

jQuery UI has an example page where you can play around with the different position settings at `http://jqueryui.com/position/`.

In the context of the tooltip, the `my` parameter specifies the position of the tooltip arrow. The following diagram shows each of the configurations for the `my` parameter:

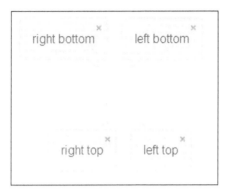

The `at` parameter for the tooltip works exactly the same way as with jQuery UI's position method.

Loading AJAX content in the tooltip widget

A commonly used pattern for tooltips is loading external content. Wijmo tooltips have the `ajaxCallback` option for inserting content into the tooltip. Our example sends a request to the server and displays its response. We set the `data-id` attribute on the links to be the indexes of the content we want. For instance, this link refers to the first element in a table:

```
<a href="#" data-id="0">link text</a>
```

Since you're sending the request to the server, `data-id` would be the primary key of the row in the table or model you're querying. The following code snippet demonstrates how to retrieve AJAX content:

```
$(document).ready(function () {
  $("a[data-id]").wijtooltip({
    position: { my: 'left bottom', at: 'right top' },
    ajaxCallback: function () {
      var $tooltip = this;
      $.get(url, { id: $tooltip.attr("data-id") }, function (text)
```

```
          {
              $tooltip.wijtooltip("option", "content", text);
          });
      }
    });
  });
```

In the `ajaxCallback` function, the ID associated with each link is retrieved with `$tooltip.attr("data-id")`, which returns the value of the `data-id` attribute. This ID is then used to retrieve the tooltip contents, which is set with `$tooltip.wijtooltip("option", "content", "text")`.

Styling the tooltip widget

By default, Wijmo styles tooltips using the theme you selected, but we want tooltips to stand out from the rest of the user interface. By applying a few CSS classes, we can quickly change a Rocket-themed tooltip to a customized tooltip as shown in the following screenshot:

When styling the tooltip, the idea is to set the border, background, and text colors without overriding the default theme classes such as `.ui-container`. We do this by setting the colors on the tooltip classes:

```
.wijmo-wijtooltip-container {
  color: #ffffff;
  background-color: slategray;
}
  .wijmo-wijtooltip-pointer-inner {
    border-right-color: slategray !important;
}
  .wijmo-wijtooltip, .wijmo-wijtooltip-pointer {
    border: 3px solid lawngreen;
}
```

The `.wijmo-wijtooltip-pointer-inner` class is applied to the tail in the speech bubble, so we set its background color to be the same as the `.wijmo-wijtooltip-container` class. The text color is also set within the `.wijmo-wijtooltip-container` class. Finally, we set the border colors on the tooltip and the pointer.

To make it easier to adjust the colors, I set the tooltip to show automatically with the `closeBehavior` option set to `sticky`. Making the tooltip sticky makes it stay on the page after moving the mouse outside of the `target` element. In this case, it's the label. The complete example is as follows:

```
<!DOCTYPE HTML>
<html>
<head>
...

  <script id="scriptInit" type="text/javascript">
    $(document).ready(function () {
      $("[title]").wijtooltip({
      modal: true
    });
      $("[title]").wijtooltip("option","closeBehavior","sticky");
        $("[title]").wijtooltip ("show");
      });
  </script>
  <style>
    .wijmo-wijtooltip-container {
      color: #ffffff;
      background-color: slategray;
  }
    .wijmo-wijtooltip-pointer-inner {
      border-right-color: slategray !important;
    }
    .wijmo-wijtooltip, .wijmo-wijtooltip-pointer {
      border: 3px solid lawngreen;
    }
    </style>
  </head>
<body>
  <label id="tooltip" title="tooltip"></label>
</body>
</html>
```

Using the upload widget with the ProgressBar element

The Wijmo `upload` widget can upload multiple files at once, and supports a progress bar. File uploads use `HttpHandler` to reduce the load on the server.

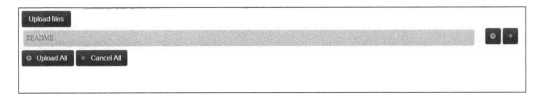

When initialized, the upload widget only has the **Upload files** button as shown in the preceding screenshot. Once a file is selected, the upload file user interface has the **Upload files** button to open the file browser, a **Cancel All** button, and an **Upload All** button. Each file that is selected has an individual upload or cancel button next to it. While uploading, the upload progress is shown in a progress bar element.

We will look at an example of replacing file inputs in web forms, where the file uploads are submitted with the form:

```
<!DOCTYPE html>
<html>
<head>

...
<script id="scriptInit" type="text/javascript">
  $(document).ready(function () {
    varprogressbar = $("#progressbar");
    //Initializes the wijupload with file-input element.
    var upload = $("#upload").wijupload({
      totalUpload: function () {
      progressbar.show();
    },
    //Hide the progress-bar when upload action finished.
    totalComplete: function () {
      progressbar.fadeOut(1500, function () {
        if (supportXhr) {
          $("#progressbar").wijprogressbar("option", "value", 0);
        }
      });
    },
```

```
        //Get the total progress of wijupload and update the
        //progress-bar.
        totalProgress: function (e, data) {
          if (supportXhr) {
            $("#progressbar").wijprogressbar("option", "maxValue",
              data.total);
            $("#progressbar").wijprogressbar("option", "value",
              data.loaded);
          }
        },
        action: $("form").attr("action")
      });
      supportXhr = $("#upload").wijupload("supportXhr");
      if (supportXhr) {
        progressbar.wijprogressbar({ value: 0 });
      }
      progressbar.hide();
    });
  </script>
  <style>
    #progressbar-container {
      height: 5em;
    }
    form {
      width: 800px;
    }
  </style>
</head>
<body>
  <form action="">
  <input id="upload" type="file" multiple/>
  <div id="progressbar-container">
  <div id="progressbar"></div>
  </div>
  </form>
</body>
</html>
```

With supportXhr = $("#upload").wijupload("supportXhr"), we check whether the upload widget can be hooked up with AJAX to display file upload progress. Although hidden, the progress bar is initialized when AJAX hooks are available.

The `upload` widget is initialized with three event handlers to enable the progress bar. First, `totalUpload` is the event that gets fired when the **Upload All** button is clicked. In this example, we show the progress bar. Since `<div id="progressbar"></div>` is an empty element, calling the jQuery `show` method does not render anything visible. Next, the `totalComplete` event is triggered when all the files have been uploaded. We fadeout the progress bar and set its value to zero for its next use. Finally, as the file is getting uploaded, the function defined for `totalProgress` receives the upload progress and the number of bytes uploaded to display in the progress bar. The `action` option for the upload widget is the URL where the form is submitted on the server.

Applying Wijmo themes to HTML5 videos

The Wijmo video widget works with the HTML5 video tag and adds controls using jQuery UI theming. The video player has the common play/stop, volume, and full-screen controls. To initialize the widget, just call the `wijvideo` method on a video element. To support all browsers, the video element needs to have the video encoded in at least two formats. The browser support for each format is as follows:

Browser	MP4	WebM	Ogg
Internet Explorer 9+	YES	NO	NO
Chrome 6+	YES	YES	YES
Firefox 3.6+	NO	YES	YES
Safari 5+	YES	NO	NO
Opera 10.6+	NO	YES	YES

For older browsers that don't support HTML5 such as IE8, it is recommended to not use the video widget. However, you can insert text content to display a message in place of the video. The full markup looks like the following:

```
<video width="520" height="340"controls="controls">
  <source src="movie.mp4" type="video/mp4">
  <source src="movie.ogg" type="video/ogg">
    Your browser does not support the video tag.
</video>
```

If you change the width or height, the video automatically resizes to fit the area. To initialize the video widget, we would call `$("video").wijvideo()`.

Using the editor widget

The Wijmo editor allows non-technical users to manage and write HTML content. Unlike other HTML editing tools for the browser on the market, Wijmo sports a Microsoft Office 2007 style Ribbon UI, as shown in the following screenshot:

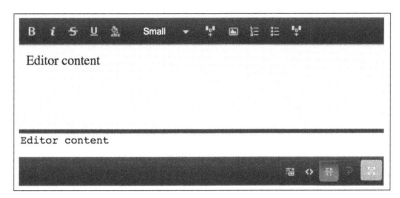

The Ribbon UI automatically resizes to fit within the textarea dimensions that create the widget, as shown in the preceding screenshot. It supports three views for editing HTML. For non-technical users, there is a **WYSIWYG** view that acts like Microsoft Word. The formatting and layout is exactly what you see in the editor. In addition, there is a source code view for those who know HTML. Furthermore, the **split** view is a combination of these two so that the HTML and its preview are both visible. To initialize an editor, just call the `wijeditor` method on a textarea; for example, `$("#wijeditor").wijeditor({ mode: "ribbon"})`.

Using the editor widget with BBCode for forums

For forum and blog use, the editor supports BBCode, namely tags such as `[url=http://example.com]Example[/url]`. If BBCode is used, the source view is in the BBCode format. The editor must be initialized in the `bbcode` mode:

```
<textarea id="wijeditor" style="width: 450px; height:
  200px;">Editor content</textarea>
```

Calling `$("#wijeditor").wijeditor({ mode: "bbcode"})` generates an editor with BBCode controls.

Summary

In this chapter, we learned about the tooltip, upload, video, and editor widgets. These widgets are commonly used in web applications. We took a look at customizing the tooltip styling so that it stands out from the rest of the UI and loading AJAX content in it. We've seen how to upload multiple files with Wijmo while showing a progress bar, a video widget, and the Ribbon style editor. In the next chapter, you will learn how to combine Wijmo with Knockout to build interactive user interfaces.

6
Dashboard with WijmoGrid

Developing rich client applications with jQuery UI results in a large number of CSS query selectors and event handlers. In this chapter, you will learn about another way of developing interactive user interfaces. Wijmo facilitates the shift to this programming paradigm, supporting it with a plugin. This chapter will get you started with the concepts.

Introduction to MVVM

Modern web applications are often built with the MVC pattern, for the backend. What about the frontend? Frameworks such as `Backbone.js` leave a lot of boilerplate code to be written. This becomes apparent for large projects. The library is lightweight, but lacks strong abstractions. It leaves the task of loading data from the server and DOM manipulation to the developer.

With the **ModelViewViewModel (MVVM)** pattern, the application logic is encapsulated in a set of ViewModel classes that expose an object model that is View-friendly. Views rely on bindings to observables to be notified of changes in the ViewModel. As a result, the UI refreshes automatically with the data when using the MVVM pattern. The flow of data in the MVVM pattern is illustrated in this diagram:

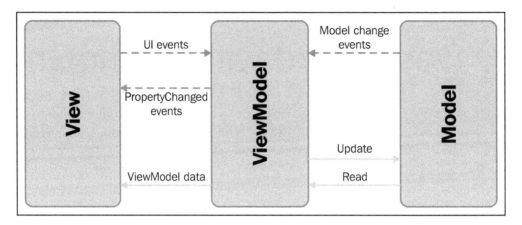

From a software design point of view, the MVVM pattern has the benefit of testability, separation of concerns, and reusability. The ViewModel doesn't contain any user interface elements, making it easy to test. The presentation is kept in the **View** with HTML and CSS, which requires different skills than those for working with the business logic in the **ViewModel**. The ViewModel can be reused in other views, such as a mobile one or in a similar application with a different look. In my own experience, I have used subclasses of a common ViewModel to build two applications. Both of the applications use the same backend **Model**.

When the MVVM pattern is used in the browser, the Model represents the backend. It is an abstraction of the normalized data store for objects and the operations (create, read, update, delete) on it. The View is the user interface that displays information to the user and fires events to the ViewModel. The ViewModel retrieves data from the Model and notifies the View of changes. Also, it receives UI events from the View and updates the data in the Model in response.

Introduction to Knockout

Knockout is a JavaScript library that implements the MVVM pattern. By using Knockout, you can avoid event handling and DOM manipulation with jQuery and work with declarative bindings instead. Knockout comes with a rich set of bindings for controlling the text, appearance, and flow. These include `foreach`, `if`, `visiblility`, and `style` bindings. In addition, there are specific bindings for working with form fields. They can be used to handle click events and to enable or disable UI elements. These bindings are bound to an observable or an `observableArray` object in the ViewModel. An observable issues notifications when their value changes. Knockout provides a simple syntax for reading and writing from an observable, as we will see. Equally important, Knockout keeps track of the right parts of your UI to update when the ViewModel changes. That means if you update an item of an `observableArray` object that is rendered with a `foreach` loop, the HTML element that corresponds to the item changes with it. If an observable is computed from another observable, then the dependency is tracked for you.

Let's take a look at instantiating and using an observable. To create an observable, we assign it to a property of a ViewModel.

```
varviewModel = {
  name: ko.observable('Bob')
};
```

To read from the observable, just call the observable with no parameters. If we call `viewModel.name()`, "Bob" is returned. To write to the observable, pass the new value as the parameter to the observable. Calling `viewModel.name('Jeff')` writes the value `Jeff` to the value `name`.

Next, we write the View with a templating language using the `data-bind` attribute:

```
My name is <span data-bind="text: name"></span>
```

The View has the same effect as the following when initialized:

```
My name is <span>Bob</span>
```

Finally, to activate Knockout, we bind the ViewModel layer to the View layer with JavaScript:

```
ko.applyBindings(myViewModel);
```

We can place this either at the bottom of the page or a DOM-ready function.

Building a rating system with Knockout

In this section we build a rating system using Wijmo's rating widget. The rating system lets the user vote for the factors that affect their technology choices. They have a total of 10 points to use. The **Finish** button is only enabled if the number of points left for use is valid as shown in the following screenshot:

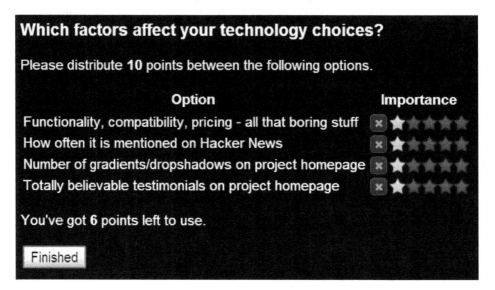

To build this rating system, we make use of Wijmo's Knockout binding for its rating widgets. The survey is composed of a set of options where the user rates the option. For each of the options, we create an answer object with the values for the binding:

```
function Answer(text) {
  this.answerText = text;
  this.points = ko.observable(1);
  this.split = ko.observable(2); // each star is split into 2
    sections to allow voting by .5
}
```

The contents of answerText are displayed under the **Option** heading. The points are the number of stars under the **Importance** heading. The rating widget has many other options, but we only introduce the ones necessary for our use. These options are bound to the widget with the data-bind attribute:

```
<div data-bind="wijrating: { value: points, split: split }"></div>
```

In our ViewModel, we have an array of options called `answers` and a total number of points allowed, the `pointsBudget`. The `pointsUsed` is a dependent observable and is calculated by adding up the points in all the answers:

```
function SurveyViewModel(pointsBudget, answers) {
  this.pointsBudget = pointsBudget;
  this.answers = $.map(answers, function (text) {
  return new Answer(text)
});
this.save = function () {
  alert('To do')
};

this.pointsUsed = ko.computed(function () {
  var total = 0;
  for (var i = 0; i <this.answers.length; i++)
    total += this.answers[i].points();
  return total;
}, this);
```

Using the jQuery `$.map` function, we can pass an array of option texts to the `SurveyViewModel`class. The first argument sets the total number of points allowed:

```
newSurveyViewModel(10, [
"Functionality, compatibility, pricing - all that boring stuff",
"How often it is mentioned on Hacker News",
"Number of gradients/dropshadows on project homepage",
"Totally believable testimonials on project homepage"
])
```

Since Knockout is an MVVM framework, we need to write the View using a templating language. To display the options and the rating widget, we loop through each answer in the ViewModel and display the `answerText` string and the points for each answer, as follows:

```
<tbody data-bind="foreach: answers">
<tr>
  <td data-bind="text: answerText"></td>
  <td><div data-bind="wijrating: { value: points, split: split
    }"></div></td>
</tr>
</tbody>
```

The `text` binding applied to `answerText` displays its text value, while the `value` binding for `wijrating` shows up as stars. Next, we want to show the number of points the user is left with. This is also done with the help of `text` binding, which converts a numeric value to a string:

```
<p>You've got <b data-bind="text: pointsBudget -
pointsUsed()"></b> points left to use.</p>
```

We enable the **Submit** button only when the value of `pointsUsed` doesn't exceed the value we set in the SurveyViewModel. In this case, it's `10`. The `click` binding assigns the `save` action in the SurveyViewModel to the `click` event on the button:

```
<button data-bind="enable: pointsUsed() <= pointsBudget, click:
save">Finished</button>
```

To initialize the UI, we bind the ViewModel to the HTML by calling `ko.applyBindings` and passing a SurveyViewModel object. Putting it all together, the rating system is only a few lines of JavaScript and has no DOM manipulation. For the complete source code for this example, refer to the code bundle available for download online on the Packt website. Note that in addition to the usual Wijmo imports, we add the Knockout library and the Wijmo bindings, which includes `wijrating`.

Now that you know how to build a user interface with the MVVM design pattern, we go on to building a more complete application with forms and grids.

Building the dashboard

The project for the rest of the chapter is based on a mobile-paging application. The application allows messages to be sent to pagers with a dashboard showing all of the messages. The messages in the dashboard are updated in real time and are sortable by column headings. In a real-world application, the messages shown in the dashboard would be paginated and sorting each column would send an AJAX request to the server. Wijmo already has an example of how to do this with the Grid widget, which we will also use in our project. Our project introduces the basics of setting up a real-time messaging platform with the MVVM pattern. The data is not persisted to a database. However, form submissions are sent to the dashboard in real time with WebSockets. After you finish this chapter, I would encourage you to take a look at `http://wijmo.com/grid-with-knockout-viewmodel-loading-remote-data/`.

Sending a message with Knockout and Socket.IO

The **Send Message** page is a form that lets the user submit a message with a subject, body, phone number, and message type. We build this form using a combination of the bindings that come with Knockout and those provided by Wijmo. First, let's start with a subject and a body. Since the Wijmo's textbox widget doesn't have a binding for the input value, we use Knockout's `value` binding. This binding can be used on the `<input>`, `<select>`, and `<textarea>` elements and links the element's value with a property in the ViewModel:

```
<ul class="formdecorator">
  <li>
    <h3> Subject </h3>
    <input id="text1" type="text" data-bind="value: subject"/>
  </li>

  <li>
    <h3> Body </h3>
    <textarea id="textarea1" rows="2" cols="50" data-bind="value:
body"></textarea>
  </li>
</ul>
```

To make these elements use the same styles as the rest of the form, we decorate them with the textbox widget. This is done for styling the elements, as the View in HTML contains the bindings:

```
$('#text1,#textarea1').wijtextbox();
```

In our ViewModel, we initialize the `subject` and `body` fields as observables with empty strings:

```
varViewModel = function () {
  this.subject = ko.observable('');
  this.body = ko.observable('');
};
```

After seeing how the `subject` and `body` fields are implemented, you may want to use the `wijtextbox` binding directly, as shown in the following demonstration that does not work:

```
<ul class="formdecorator">
  <li>
    <h3> Subject </h3>
    <input id="text1" type="text" data-bind="wijtextbox:
      {value: subject}"/>
  </li>
  <li>
    <h3> Body </h3>
    <textarea id="Textarea1" rows="2" cols="50" databind="wijtextbox:
      {value: body}">
    </textarea>
  </li>
</ul>
```

Although Knockout has a `value` binding, the `wijtextbox` binding is purely for presentation. For a list of supported options for each binding, see `http://wijmo.com/wiki/index.php/Using_Wijmo_with_Knockout`. Only the options listed on the page support two-way bindings while other widget options are just used for initialization. In the next step, Wijmo bindings are used for the phone number and message type form components:

```
<li>
  <h3> Phone Number </h3>
  <input data-bind="wijinputmask:
    { text: phoneNumber, mask: '(999) 000-0000' }" />
</li>

<li>
  <h3> Message Type </h3>
  <input data-bind="wijcombobox:
    { text: messageType, data: messageTypes }"/>
</li>
```

The `wijinputmask` binding initializes a `WijmoInputMask` widget with the pattern (___) ___-____. The `text` option binds it to the observable `phoneNumber` in the ViewModel. The `wijcombobox` widget acts as a dropdown for the message type. The `data` option sets the `messageTypes` as available. Since the message types are only read and not written, we scope it outside of the ViewModel. Changes to objects outside of the ViewModel layer do not affect the UI. Later on, we submit the ViewModel object to the server and having extraneous data such as message types outside of the ViewModel layer simplifies the code. Wijmo's ComboBox takes an array of objects with the label and value for the data option. The `label` property is the text displayed, while `value` would be stored in the `messageType` observable.

```
varmessageTypes = $.map(["Alpha", "Beta", "Gamma"], function (type)
{
  return {label: type, value: type}
});
```

To initialize the message type to `Gamma`, we set it in the observable:

```
varViewModel = function () {
  this.subject = ko.observable('');
  this.body = ko.observable('');
  this.messageType = ko.observable('Gamma');
  this.phoneNumber = ko.observable('');
};
```

Finally, the last item we have left on the form is a submit button which sends the data to the server using a WebSocket object. For this part, we will use Socket.IO. To set up `Socket.IO`, download and install `Node.JS` from `http://nodejs.org/download/`, then run `npm install socket.io` on the command line. This will make the path `/socket.io/socket.io.js` available in the browser when the `Node.JS` server is running. On the server, `Socket.IO` listens for message events and broadcasts it as news. The `emit` function broadcasts to all clients except the one who sent the message:

```
io.sockets.on('connection', function (socket) {
  socket.on('message', function (data) {
  socket.broadcast.emit('news', data);
  });
});
```

In the browser, a WebSocket connection is created to `localhost` by calling `io.connect('http://localhost')`. The `submit` function sends a message event to the server:

```
varViewModel = function () {
...
  this.submit = function () {
    socket.emit('message', ko.toJSON(viewModel));
  }
};
```

`ko.toJSON` converts the ViewModel data to JSON. JSON includes all of the observables. The submit button is bound to the method through the click binding:

```
<li>
  <button id="Button1" data-bind="click: submit">
    Submit
  </button>
</li>
```

For decorating the button, call `$('button').button()`. The jQuery UI button method styles the submit button in the same way as other widgets. You may ask, why not just write the View so that the jQuery UI button is applied in the binding? The following code would work in a perfect world:

```
<button id="Button1" data-bind="button: { click: submit }">
  Submit
</button>
```

Yet, Wijmo does not support binding to the `click` event on button widgets. So we use Knockout's native `click` binding and jQuery UI's `button` method.

To make the View and the ViewModel layers work together, we apply the bindings to the HTML:

```
varviewModel = new ViewModel();
ko.applyBindings(viewModel);
```

With the Rocket theme, the **Send Message** page looks like the following screenshot:

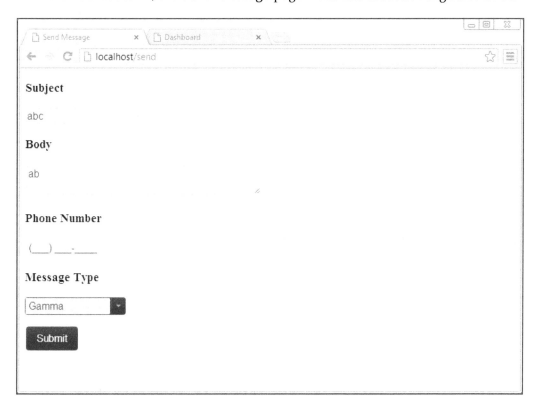

Displaying messages on the Dashboard

Our ViewModel class for the Dashboard page is simple. It is composed of an `observableArray` of message objects. An `observableArray` is useful when you want to detect and respond to changes in a collection of JavaScript objects. Since the messages on the Dashboard are not editable, the properties of each message object do not need to be an observable. Each message has `subject`, `body`, `messageType`, and, `phoneNumber` strings:

```
varviewModel = {
  data: ko.observableArray([
    {"subject": "Hi", "body": "Just a message", "messageType":
      "Gamma", "phoneNumber": "4128675309"}
  ])
};
```

On receiving an update from the server, the message is added to the ViewModel. The data is received as text, as in AJAX responses. So the `JSON.parse` method turns it into a `message` object:

```
var socket = io.connect('http://localhost');
socket.on('news', function (data) {
  viewModel.data.push(JSON.parse(data));
});
```

In the preceding code, a WebSocket connection is made to the server, allowing bi-directional communication. However, we only listen for events from the server for the Dashboard.

Our View layer is just a table. Wijmo makes displaying tabular data so easy that all we need to make it dynamic is just the `wijgrid` binding, along with one essential option, `data`. The `data` option takes as its parameter a `wijdatasource` widget, an array, or a DOM table. A `wijdatasource` can be used to load data dynamically from a remote source with filtering and sorting. Because our application doesn't have a database in the Model, we pass an `observableArray` to the `data` option:

```
<table id="dataGrid" data-bind="wijgrid: { data: data,
  allowSorting: true }">
</table>
```

To enhance the functionality, `allowSorting` is set so that clicking on a column heading sorts the table by that column. The `wijgrid` binding takes care of updating the table when the ViewModel data changes. As you are now familiar, we are missing an essential piece that links the View and the ViewModels: `ko.applyBindings(viewModel)`. That finishes the dashboard with the result as seen in the following screenshot:

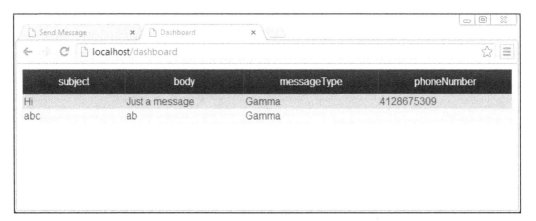

The dashboard initially loads with just the first message. When the **Send Message** page is submitted, another message is inserted below it.

Summary

Wijmo, combined with Knockout, makes programming interactive applications easy. In the rating system example, we have seen how observables that are computed from other observables work. We've used a dependent observable to calculate the total number of points used as each rating changes. In the Dashboard example, we built a dynamic table that is updated by the server with the Wijmo grid widget. Also, we coded the Send Message page to use the Wijmo widgets in combination with Knockout bindings. The next chapter introduces mobile web development with Wijmo Mobile.

7
Wijmo Mobile

Introduced in the 2013 release, adaptive widgets can be used in both desktop and mobile web applications. In this chapter, we take a quick tour of Wijmo mobile: the setup, simple widgets, and views. In particular, we focus on the AppView, Wijmo's adaptive super widget that lets you use the same pages for mobile and desktop browsers.

Getting started with Wijmo mobile

In this section, I show you how to enable Wijmo's mobile widgets. We go through the steps of obtaining jQuery mobile and creating widgets. Wijmo mobile widgets are an extension of jQuery's mobile widgets. I also explain how a different approach to creating mobile widgets is taken by jQuery mobile.

Setting up Wijmo mobile

Since Wijmo mobile is built on jQuery mobile, we will first obtain and install jQuery mobile.

Obtaining jQuery mobile

You will need to replace the jQuery UI library used in the setup previously with jQuery mobile, which is available from `http://jquerymobile.com/download/`. jQuery mobile also has a Theme Roller like jQuery UI. The default theme is included in the jQuery mobile package. If you want to make a custom theme, you can do so at `http://jquerymobile.com/themeroller/`.

Installing jQuery mobile

You need to copy over the following items from the jQuery mobile download into the `lib` folder:

* The `jquery.mobile-1.3.1.min.js` file
* The `jquery.mobile-1.3.1.min.css` file for the CSS styles
* The images directory for jQuery mobile icons

Once the files are in place, a mobile page can be created. In the following code snippet, I show the contents of an example page using jQuery mobile:

```
<!DOCTYPE HTML>
<HTML>
<head>
<meta name="viewport" content="width=device-width"/>
<!--jQuery References-->
<script src="../lib/jquery-1.9.1.js"
  type="text/javascript"></script>
<script src="../lib/jquery.mobile-1.3.1.min.js"
  type="text/javascript"></script>
<!--Wijmo Widgets JavaScript-->
<script src="../lib/jquery.wijmo-open.all.3.20131.2.js"
  type="text/javascript"></script>
<script src="../lib/jquery.wijmo-pro.all.3.20131.2.js"
  type="text/javascript"></script>
<!--Theme-->
<link href="../lib/jquery.mobile-1.3.1.min.css" rel="stylesheet"
  type="text/css"/>
<!--Wijmo Widgets CSS-->
<link href="../lib/jquery.wijmo-open.3.20131.2.css"
  rel="stylesheet" type="text/css"/>
<link href="../lib/jquery.wijmo-pro.3.20131.2.css"
  rel="stylesheet" type="text/css"/>
</head>
<body>
  <div data-role="page" data-theme="b">
  <div data-role="content">
  <div data-role="header">
  <h1>Page Title</h1>
  </div>
  <div data-role="content">
  <button>Press Here</button>
  </div>
```

```
      </div>
      </div>
   </body>
   </HTML>
```

Instead of the jQuery UI library, we used jQuery mobile here. In addition, we replaced the Wijmo Rocket theme with the jQuery UI theme.

Using a mobile browser emulator

For this chapter, we use the Opera mobile emulator available at `http://www.opera.com/developer/mobile-emulator`. Compared to the iPhone or Android emulators, it is easier to install and simulate different devices with different screen sizes. The Opera mobile browser is also widely used and supported on all popular platforms. The following screenshot shows you the previous example of a jQuery mobile page rendered in Opera mobile:

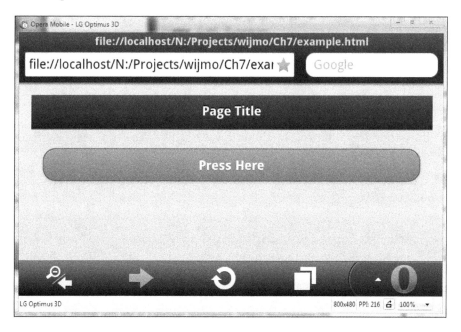

Creating an expander widget

The expander is for collapsible content. Unlike the accordion, it only has a single section. To create an expander, wrap the collapsible block in a single-parent element and apply the `data-role="wijexpander" attribute` to the parent element. You can see how to do this in the following example, where only the contents of the `body` tag are shown:

```
<div data-role="page" data-theme="b">
<div data-role="content">
<div data-role="wijexpander">
<h3>Header</h3>

<div>
Loremipsum...
</div>
</div>
</div>
</div>
```

The default for an expander shows the content within the block.

Passing options to the expander widget

To make the expander collapsed by default, we use the `data-options` attribute and set `expanded` to `false`.

```
<div data-role="wijexpander" data-options='{ expanded: false }'>
<h3>Header</h3>

<div>
...
</div>
</div>
```

Since Wijmo mobile is still new, many of the widgets do not have mobile counterparts and a few of the options supported for desktop browsers don't work. Namely, the option `contentUrl` does not work in the 3.20131.2 version, and setting the expand direction to `right` makes the UI look confusing. Here, we see an example of changing the expand direction by setting `data-options='{expandDirection: "right"}'`:

Creating a ListView widget

The ListView acts as a list of links for navigation. jQuery mobile applies the necessary styles to make the list mobile-friendly. Once a list item is tapped on, the link content is loaded through AJAX and inserted into the page. This improves the user perception as they do not see a blank screen. A ListView is created by setting the `data-role` attribute of an HTML list to `listview` with each list item containing a link:

```
<div data-role="page">
<div data-role="content">
<ul data-role="listview" data-autodividers="true" data-theme="c">
<li><a href="http://wijmo.com/demos/">Wijmo Demos</a></li>
<li><a
href="http://wijmo.com/wiki/index.php/ListView">WijmoListView
Documentation</a></li>
<li><a href="http://jquerymobile.com/demos/1.2.0/docs/lists/docs-
lists.html">jQuery Mobile Lists</a></li>
</ul>
</div>
</div>
```

With `data-autodividers="true"` on the list parent, the list items are categorized by their first letter. The list items show up as navigation buttons with right arrows as shown in the following screenshot:

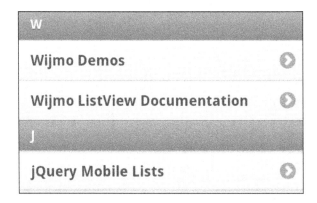

Creating an AppView widget

The WijmoAppView creates a responsive layout that adapts to the screen size. It works similar to ListView on phones. On desktops and tablets, the list is displayed on the left side with the content pane taking up the rest of the page. Note that when using AppView, your jQuery mobile and jQuery versions must be compatible with the release of Wijmo you're using. For this example, I am using jQuery 1.8.2, jQuery mobile 1.2.0, and Wijmo3.20131.4.

An AppView is composed of an AppView page and a ListView for navigation:

```
<div data-role="wijappview">
<div data-role="appviewpage">
<div data-role="header" data-position="fixed">
<h2>Title</h2>
</div>
<div data-role="content">
<h3>Content for Tablets</h3>
<p>On an tablet the AppView will result in a multi-column layout
with an always visible menu. This view is optimized for tablets
or even full desktop browsers. AppView will automatically use
this view when running on a large enough screen.</p>
</div>
<div data-role="footer" data-position="fixed">
<h2>Footer</h2>
</div>
```

```
  </div>
  <div data-role="menu" class="ui-body-a">
  <ul data-role="listview" data-theme="a">
    <li><a href="calendar.html">Calendar</a></li>
    <li><a href="form.html">Form</a></li>
    <li><a href="accordion.html">Accordion</a></li>
  </ul>
  </div>
  </div>
```

Under the AppView page, the page title is set in an element using `data-role="header"`, which is always displayed at the top of the page. As you might guess, there is also a `data-role="footer"` attribute, which is displayed at the bottom of the page when data-position is set to `fixed`. The content area in the preceding code marked with `data-role="content"` only shows in tablets. You can see how the page would look like in a tablet in the following screenshot:

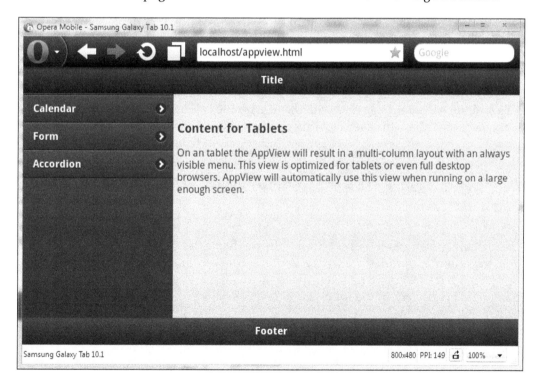

The navigation panel is a ListView widget wrapped around by a `data-role="menu"` element. On the phone, only the navigation panel is shown when the AppView is loaded as in the following screenshot:

To make the menu items work, we need to serve the files set in the `href` attributes from a server since they are loaded through AJAX. The downloadable source code for this chapter includes a file server written in `Node.JS`.

Adding the AppView pages

Let's add the calendar page and initialize it with the calendar widget. Create a `calendar.html` file with the following code:

```
<div data-role="appviewpage" data-title="Calendar">
  <div data-role="content">
    <div id="wijcalendar" data-role="wijcalendar"></div>
  </div>
</div>
```

The contents under `data-role="content"` are displayed in the content area. In this area, the calendar is added by setting `data-role="wijcalendar"` on a `div`. On the top left is a **Back** button, which returns to the main menu. It is added whenever a menu item is selected. In the following screen, I selected the calendar menu entry:

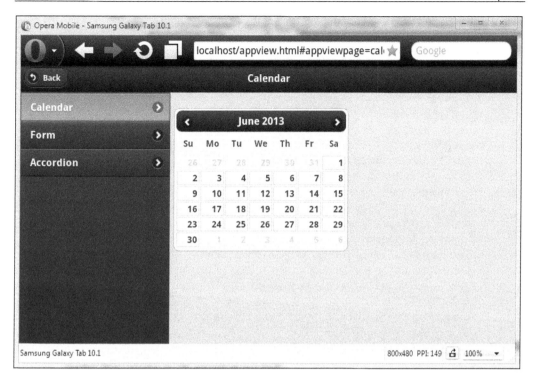

If the example doesn't work for you, the first thing to try is replacing the header styles and scripts with the ones hosted on the CDN: `http://wijmo.com/downloads/#wijmo-cdn`. The next step is to upload your HTML files and post a question on the forum `http://wijmo.com/forums/`. In addition, check the AJAX requests and make sure your files are being served locally.

Reusing non-mobile pages

Suppose we already have a `calendar.html` file. How can it be used with the new mobile app? You just need to add `data-role="appviewpage"`, `data-role="content"`, and insert `data-role="widgetname"` for all widgets on the page. For instance, we could replace `calendar.html` with the following, keeping the reference to jQuery UI and the Rocket theme:

```
<!DOCTYPE HTML>
<html>
<head>
```

```
<title>Calendar</title>
<!--jQuery References-->
<script src="../lib/jquery-1.9.1.js"
  type="text/javascript"></script>
<script src="../lib/jquery-ui.custom.js"
  type="text/javascript"></script>
<!--Wijmo Widgets JavaScript-->
<script src="../lib/jquery.wijmo-open.all.js"
  type="text/javascript"></script>
<script src="../lib/jquery.wijmo-pro.all.3.20131.2.js"
  type="text/javascript"></script>
<!--Theme-->
<link href="../lib/jquery-wijmo.css" rel="stylesheet"
  type="text/css" />
<!--Wijmo Widgets CSS-->
<link href="../lib/jquery.wijmo-open.css" rel="stylesheet"
  type="text/css" />
<link href="../lib/jquery.wijmo-pro.3.20131.2.css"
  rel="stylesheet" type="text/css" />
<script id="scriptInit" type="text/javascript">
  $(document).ready(function () {
    $('#wijcalendar').wijcalendar()
  });
</script>
</head>
<body>
  <div data-role="appviewpage">
  <div data-role="content">
  <div id="wijcalendar" data-role="wijcalendar"></div>
  </div>
  </div>
</body>
</html>
```

We added two extra elements for the required data-roles. Your page may have a different structure and you may just need to add the `data-roles` attribute to existing elements. The JavaScript on the page is not executed, as Wijmo ignores everything except the title outside of `data-role="appviewpage"`. Since the title is set with `<title>Calendar</title>`, Wijmo uses it as the title for the page as shown in the following screenshot:

On desktop browsers, the page still displays the calendar widget. Take a look at the screenshot:

This is quite remarkable as jQuery mobile does not have a similar widget to allow reuse of non-mobile pages. Using the WijmoAppView, separate mobile development is no longer necessary.

Summary

This chapter introduced Wijmo mobile widgets. Unlike jQuery mobile, Wijmo's adaptive widgets can be used on both desktops and phones. We started by setting up the development environment, then we looked at several widgets, starting from the simplest.

8
Extending Wijmo

In this chapter, I show you how to modify Wijmo's widgets and CSS styles for themes. You will learn how to add a button to the dialog widget without overriding existing buttons. Then, I introduce an easy way to modify existing Wijmo themes.

Extending Wijmo Open

Wijmo Open is a set of open source jQuery UI widgets. Wijmo widgets such as the slider, dialog, or accordion are extensions to jQuery UI's widgets. Others, such as Wijmo's menu or dropdown, are new widgets.

Modifying the Dialog widget

In *Chapter 2*, *The Dialog Widget*, I showed you how to add custom buttons to the dialog widget without changing the internals. The API is unwieldy, in that you must override the icons and behavior for a default button. Now, I will show you how to add a custom button by extending the API. First, open `jquery.wijmo-open.all.js` and rename it as `jquery.wijmo-open.all.extended.js`.

When you open `jquery.wijmo-open.all.extended.js` in an editor, use code folding to collapse all the code and search for `wijdialog`. You will get a view that looks like the following screenshot after expanding on the line with `varWijDialog`:

```
/*...*/
/*...*/
var wijmo;
(function (wijmo) {...})(wijmo || (wijmo = {}));
;
var __extends = this.__extends || function (d, b) {...};
/// <reference path="../Base/jquery.wijmo.widget.ts"/>
/*...*/
/*...*/
var wijmo;
(function (wijmo) {
    "use strict";
    var $ = jQuery, widgetName = "wijdialog", uiStateHover = "ui-state-hover", zonCSS = "wijmo-wijdialog
    var WijDialog = (function (_super) {
        __extends(WijDialog, _super);
        function WijDialog() {...}
        WijDialog.prototype._create = function () {...};
        WijDialog.prototype._init = function () {...};
        WijDialog.prototype._makeDraggable = function () {...};
        WijDialog.prototype._handleDisabledOption = function (disabled, ele) {...};
        WijDialog.prototype._createDisabledDiv = function () {...};
        WijDialog.prototype.destroy = function () {...};
        WijDialog.prototype._attachDraggableResizableEvent = function () {...};
        WijDialog.prototype._createIframeMask = //fixed iframe bug.
        function () {...};
        WijDialog.prototype._destoryIframeMask = function () {...};
        WijDialog.prototype._initWijWindow = function () {...};
        WijDialog.prototype._checkUrl = function () {...};
        WijDialog.prototype._setOption = function (key, value) {...};
        WijDialog.prototype._createCaptionButtons = function () {
            var captionButtons = [], self = this, o = self.options, i, buttons = {
                pin: {
                    visible: true,
                    click: self.pin,
                    iconClassOn: "ui-icon-pin-w",
                    iconClassOff: "ui-icon-pin-s"
                },
                refresh: {"visible": true...},
                toggle: {
                    visible: true,
```

All of the Wijmo Open widgets start with `"use strict"`. This turns on strict semantics for ECMAScript 5 and allows code to run faster on browsers that support it. Let's take a look at those lines that start with `WijDialog.prototype`. All the methods that start with an underscore are private, while the other ones are accessible through the API and documented. Under the `_createCaptionButtons` function, there is a `button` object with all the buttons on the title bar. To add a `hint` button to the dialog title bar, we use the same format as the other buttons:

```
varcaptionButtons = [], self = this, o = self.options, i, buttons = {
    pin: {
```

```
      visible: true,
      click: self.pin,
      iconClassOn: "ui-icon-pin-w",
      iconClassOff: "ui-icon-pin-s"
    },
    refresh: {
      visible: true,
      click: self.refresh,
      iconClassOn: "ui-icon-refresh"
    },
    toggle: {
      visible: true,
      click: self.toggle,
      iconClassOn: "ui-icon-carat-1-n",
      iconClassOff: "ui-icon-carat-1-s"
    },
    hint: {
      visible: true,
      click: self.hint,
      message: "",
      iconClassOn: "ui-icon-lightbulb"
    },
    minimize: {
      visible: true,
      click: self.minimize,
      iconClassOn: "ui-icon-minus"
    },
    maximize: {
      visible: true,
      click: self.maximize,
      iconClassOn: "ui-icon-extlink"
    },
    close: {
      visible: true,
      click: self.close,
      iconClassOn: "ui-icon-close"
    }
  }
}
```

 "use strict" may cause unexpected behavior in your code. You may want to check with a utility such as JSHint (http://www.jshint.com/) or remove strict mode altogether.

The click event for the button is specified with the `click` option. For the hint button, use `self.hint`. So, we write the `hint` function as a `WijDialog` method:

```
WijDialog.prototype.hint = function () {
  var self = this, o = self.options;
  alert(o.message);
};
```

In this function, the options are read from `self.options`, and the message string set in the option is used in an alert box. To use the new API for the hint button, we just need to set the message option:

```
$('#dialog').wijdialog({message: 'Success! You just added a title
bar button.'});
```

Be sure to change the reference to the `jquery.wijmo-open.all.js` script to `jquery.wijmo-open.all.extended.js`.

Modifying a Wijmo theme with ThemeRoller

To modify an existing Wijmo theme, open the `jquery-wijmo.css` file in the `lib` folder in our project structure. You can find more themes in your Wijmo download under the `Themes` folder. Once you've opened up the CSS file, search for `jQuery UI CSS Framework`. There should be a comment section like the following:

```
/*
 * jQuery UI CSS Framework 1.8.7
 *
 * Copyright 2010, AUTHORS.txt (http://jqueryui.com/about)
 * Dual licensed under the MIT or GPL Version 2 licenses.
 * http://jquery.org/license
 *
 * http://docs.jquery.com/UI/Theming/API
 *
 * To view and modify this theme, visit
http://jqueryui.com/themeroller/?ffDefault=...
 */
```

When you visit the link in the browser, ThemeRoller loads the Wijmo theme. The theme settings can be caned under the **Roll Your Own** tab on the left side. You can see the Rocket theme loaded in ThemeRoller in the following screenshot:

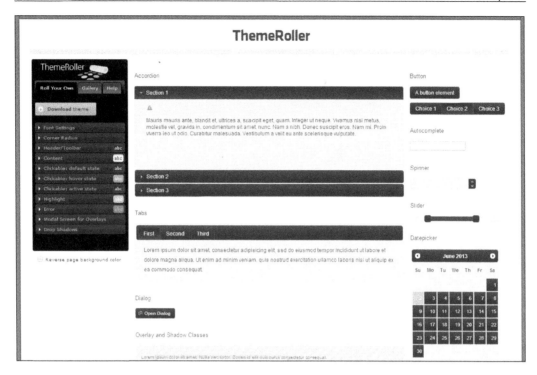

For details on how to modify a theme, see `http://wijmo.com/wiki/index.php/`
`Wijmo_Loves_ThemeRoller:_An_Overview`.

Summary

Now that you have a sense of how to change things in Wijmo, you're in a better
position to use Wijmo in your projects. Often, the situation requires changes to
the theme or the behavior of widgets. Wijmo makes it easy to make those changes.

Index

Symbols

$.map function 69
_createCaptionButtons function 92
.wijmo-wijdialog class 22
.wijmo-wijtooltip-pointer-inner class 59

A

action option 62
ajaxCallback function 58
ajaxCallback option 57
anchor element 51
animation
  URL 44
answerText string 69
AppView pages
  adding 86, 87
AppView widget
  AppView pages, adding 86, 87
  creating 84-86
  non-mobile pages, reusing 87-89
at field 56
auto option 46
autoplay
  adding 46

B

Back button 86
BBCode
  editor, using 63
blur event 16
body tag 82
buttonCreating method 16
button method 74

button object 92

C

Cancel All button 60
captionButtons option 15-17, 20
Carousel widget
  autoplay, adding 46
  configuring 41
  creating 39-41
  display options, using to show multiple
      pages 42-44
  navigation options, specifying 44, 45
  timer, adding 46
  using 39
CDN 6
changed option 28
checkbox widget 25, 26
checked attribute 26
checked property 28
clear button 36
click event 70, 74
click option 18, 94
closeBehavior option 59
ComboBox 30, 31
Content Distribution Networks. *See* CDN
contentUrl option 16, 23
controlsPosition property 52
CSS
  for Widgets, URL 7
ctrlButtons option 52
Cupertino
  URL 6
custom buttons
  adding 18-20

D

dashboard
building 70
messages, displaying 75-77
message, sending with Knockout 71-75
message, sending with Socket.IO 71-75
data-bind attribute 67, 68
data-id attribute 57, 58
data option 73, 76
data-options attribute 82
data-role attribute 83
dateFormat option 33
destroy method 30
development
jQuery UI, installing for 11
Wijmo, installing for 11
dialog appearance
configuring 21, 22
dialog widget
modifying 91-94
Wijmo, adding to 15-18
disable method 16
display options
used, to show multiple pages 42-44
div element 21
dropdown 28-30

E

editor widget
used, with BBCode for forums 63
using 63
emit function 73
expander widget
creating 82
options, passing to 82
expandingAnimation option 16
external content
loading 23

F

Finish button 68
form components
checkbox widget 25, 26
ComboBox 30, 31
dropdown 28-30

InputDate widget 31-33
InputMask widget 34-37
radio buttons 26-28
Free Trial button 10

G

gallery widget
creating 47, 48
using 46
videos, playing 49
getState method 17

H

hint button 92
hint function 94
href attribute 86
HTML5 videos
Wijmo themes, applying to 62
HTML document
Wijmo, adding to 12

I

img element 52
InputDate widget 31-33
input element 31, 32
InputMask widget
about 34-37
URL 34

J

jQuery.Event object 28
jQuery mobile
installing 80
obtaining 79
URL 79
jQuery UI
customizing, for download 9
download page, URL 9
installing, for download 11
jQuery UI 1.10.2
URL 6
jQuery UI effects
URL 31
jQuery UI icons

URL 18
JSHint
    URL 93
JSON.parse method 76

K

Knockout
    about 67
    messages, sending with 71-75
    rating system, building with 68-70

L

label property 73
lightBox widget
    appearance, changing 52
    creating 51, 52
    using 50
ListView widget
    creating 83, 84
loop option 46

M

maximize method 16
message object 76
minimize method 16
mobile browser emulator
    using 81
Model 66
ModelViewViewModel (MVVM) 66
my field 56
my option 44
my parameter 57

N

navigation options
    specifying 44, 45
Node.JS
    URL 73
non-mobile pages
    reusing 87-89

O

observableArray object 67
of field 56

offset field 56
Opera mobile emulator
    URL 81

P

pagerType option 44
pin method 16
position settings
    URL 57
ProgressBar element
    upload widget, using with 60-62

R

radio buttons 26-28
rating system
    building, with Knockout 68-70
refresh method 16, 30
rel attribute 51
reset button 37
reset method 16
restore method 16
Rocket theme
    URL 7

S

select element 29
setText method 36
showCaption option 49
showTrigger option 32
SimpleDateFormat class 33
Socket.IO
    messages, sending with 71-75
stack option 16
stateChanged event 17
Submit button 70
Submit function 74
SurveyViewModelclass 69

T

target element 59
text binding 70
text option 73
theme
    modifying, URL 95

Theme Explorer
  URL 6
ThemeRoller
  URL 9, 79
  Wijmo theme, modifying with 94, 95
thumbsDisplay option 49
thumbsLength option 49
timer
  adding 46
timer option 46
title attribute 21, 55
title option 21
toggle method 16
tooltip widget
  AJAX content, loading 57, 58
  positioning 56, 57
  styling 58, 59
  using 55
totalComplete event 62

U

Upload All button 60, 62
Upload files button 60
upload widget
  used, with ProgressBar element 60-62

V

videos
  playing, in gallery widget 49
View 66
ViewModel 66
visible option 17

W

widget method 16
width attribute 52
width option 29
wijcarousel element 42
wijdatasource widget 76
WijDialog method 17, 94
wijdropdown method 29
wijgallery method 47, 50
wijlightbox method 52

Wijmo
  adding, to dialog widget 15-18
  adding, to HTML document 12
  custom buttons, adding 18-20
  dialog appearance, configuring 21, 22
  downloading 10, 11
  external content, loading 23
  installing, for development 9-11
  installing, via CDN 6-8
  licensing 13, 14
  setting up 5
WijmoInputMask widget 73
Wijmo, installing
  jQuery UI, customizing for download 9
  jQuery UI, installing for development 11
Wijmo mobile
  jQuery mobile, installing 80
  jQuery mobile, obtaining 79
  mobile browser emulator, using 81
  setting up 79
Wijmo Open
  Dialog widget, modifying 91-94
  extending 91
  Wijmo theme, modifying with
    ThemeRoller 94, 95
Wijmo themes
  applying, to HTML5 videos 62
  modifying, with ThemeRoller 94, 95
wijradiomethod method 27

Z

zIndex option 16

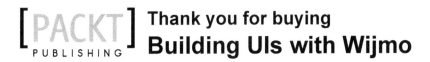
Thank you for buying
Building UIs with Wijmo

About Packt Publishing

Packt, pronounced 'packed', published its first book "*Mastering phpMyAdmin for Effective MySQL Management*" in April 2004 and subsequently continued to specialize in publishing highly focused books on specific technologies and solutions.

Our books and publications share the experiences of your fellow IT professionals in adapting and customizing today's systems, applications, and frameworks. Our solution based books give you the knowledge and power to customize the software and technologies you're using to get the job done. Packt books are more specific and less general than the IT books you have seen in the past. Our unique business model allows us to bring you more focused information, giving you more of what you need to know, and less of what you don't.

Packt is a modern, yet unique publishing company, which focuses on producing quality, cutting-edge books for communities of developers, administrators, and newbies alike. For more information, please visit our website: www.packtpub.com.

Writing for Packt

We welcome all inquiries from people who are interested in authoring. Book proposals should be sent to author@packtpub.com. If your book idea is still at an early stage and you would like to discuss it first before writing a formal book proposal, contact us; one of our commissioning editors will get in touch with you.

We're not just looking for published authors; if you have strong technical skills but no writing experience, our experienced editors can help you develop a writing career, or simply get some additional reward for your expertise.

Instant Wijmo Widgets How-to

ISBN: 978-1-782161-86-8   Paperback: 82 pages

Learn how to use Wijmo tools to speed up UI development and browser compatibility through practical recipes

1. Learn something new in an Instant! A short, fast, focused guide delivering immediate results.

2. Make calendars, sliders, dynamic and animated charts quickly and easily

3. Create a live stream chart displaying real time data

jQuery UI 1.8: The User Interface Library for jQuery

ISBN: 978-1-849516-52-5   Paperback: 424 pages

Build highly interactive web applications with ready-to-use widgets from the jQuery User Interface Library

1. Packed with examples and clear explanations of how to easily design elegant and powerful front-end interfaces for your web applications

2. A section covering the widget factory including an in-depth example on how to build a custom jQuery UI widget

3. Updated code with significant changes and fixes to the previous edition

Please check **www.PacktPub.com** for information on our titles

WordPress Multisite Administration

ISBN: 978-1-783282-47-0   Paperback: 106 pages

A concise guide to set up, manage, and customize your blog network using WordPress multisite

1. Learn how to configure a complete, functional, and attractive WordPress Multisite

2. Customize your sites with WordPress themes and plugins

3. Set up, maintain, and secure your blog network

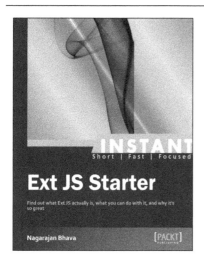

Instant Ext JS Starter

ISBN: 978-1-782166-10-8   Paperback: 56 pages

Find out what Ext JS actually is, what you can do with it, and why it's so great

1. Learn something new in an Instant!
    A short, fast, focused guide delivering immediate results

2. Install and set up the environment with this quick Starter guide

3. Learn the basics of the framework and built-in utility functions

Please check **www.PacktPub.com** for information on our titles